FEDERAL FINANCES
in the
COMING DECADE

Prepared under the Auspices of the Columbia University Council for Research in the Social Sciences

CARL SHOUP

FEDERAL FINANCES *in the* COMING DECADE

Some Cumulative Possibilities, 1941-51

NEW YORK: MORNINGSIDE HEIGHTS
COLUMBIA UNIVERSITY PRESS
1941

Foreign Agents: oxford university press, Humphrey Milford, Amen House, London, E.C., 4, England, and B. I. Building, Nicol Road, Bombay, India; maruzen company, ltd., 6 Nihonbashi, Tori-Nichome, Tokyo, Japan

MANUFACTURED IN THE UNITED STATES OF AMERICA

PREFACE

THE MATERIAL in this book was first developed for use in my course on fiscal policy at Columbia University. With the aid of a grant from the Columbia Council for Research in the Social Sciences, additional data were gathered and the material was prepared for publication. I am grateful to the Council for this help, and to my friends whose time and information I have drawn upon so extensively. Some of the observations made in the sections on borrowing, for which no specific source is given, reflect information obtained in discussion with officials in the savings bank, commercial bank, and insurance fields. Mr. George E. Lent was engaged throughout the study in checking the material, the approach used, and the reasoning involved, and has been very helpful in all these respects.

It may be an imposition on the reader to hand him a volume containing sets of figures some of which represent situations highly improbable, if not impossible, without at the same time venturing to say which combination is the most likely and attempting to prove it. But the chief aim in the present case is not outright prediction; it is instead the gaining of some sense of proportion, some sense of the size of the fiscal problem that is facing the United States. The problem is surely not too difficult to be solved with a reasonable degree of success—but the solution, whatever it may turn out to be, will not be found unless the problem is approached with a full realization of its size and its complexity and the relative importance of its various parts. Figures of some sort, even if only rough and preliminary, must be set down before this realization can be gained.

The wide range of possibilities suggested by quantities like those in this study can perhaps be narrowed enough so that policy decisions can be made with some assurance. This involves refining some of the current theories, or developing new ones, concerning the effects of expenditures, taxation, and changes in public debt as they may occur in the United States over the coming years. Fiscal theory of this kind has developed greatly in the past decade, yet not enough to give the assurance needed. "Theory" here means generalizations to which quantities can be attached, not vague statements of possible tendencies under assumptions that do not fit closely the particular situation at hand. The development of such theory is proceeding in several quarters, both within and outside the government. It has been deliberately set aside in this study, which is devoted solely to the preliminary task of gaining some notion of the possible quantities and proportions that might be involved.

The reader is warned, in several places, that the whole structure of the present discussion rests on the fundamental assumption that the particular fiscal alternative that is selected will be one that does not allow the price level to rise more than the modest amounts assumed in Table 3 yet does not prevent business activity from reaching the levels implied by the national income figures in that table. Just which fiscal policy would assure this, how expenditures and revenues would change if this aim were not achieved, the chances of a rise in prices after the war—these and other pressing problems require, as indicated above, a set of analytical tools and data much more complex and of broader scope than those utilized in the present work.

All of the data in this volume are fully available to the

public. In view of the fact that I have been engaged occasionally in research with the Federal Treasury, it is desirable to point out that the Treasury is in no way, directly or indirectly, connected with or responsible for this study. In particular, the hypothetical rate schedules shown for the income tax and estate tax were constructed solely by me, for use in my University course, and have no connection with the work that the Treasury or the Congressional experts have done on these subjects.

Carl Shoup

Columbia University
June, 1941

CONTENTS

TABLES

FEDERAL FINANCES

in the

COMING DECADE

Chapter I

A SUMMARY VIEW

THE AIM OF this study is neither to predict nor to prescribe, but to promote a careful, dispassionate discussion of Federal fiscal policy. There is still time for discussion before important and irrevocable decisions must be made. The future at this moment (June, 1941) is so obscure that no positive commitment to a long-term fiscal program can be expected until some months have passed. On the other hand, it must be remembered that even in the absence of such a commitment some decisions must be made, if only on a short-term basis, and the mere passage of time may render many of them irrevocable.

Much has already been written on financing the defense of the United States; the reasons for adding the present contribution are that (1) the alternative courses of action open to the Federal government in fiscal policy need to be presented in quantitative terms, in a much more detailed manner than has hitherto been the case, and (2) the span of time to be considered in those quantitative terms must be greater than two or three years. Without quantitative expression, the relative importance of an issue becomes blurred, and attention may be concentrated on what proves after all to be a matter of no great consequence. For example, how do the mutual savings banks compare in importance with individual savers as a possible market for future issues of Federal bonds? How do possible increases in the excise taxes compare, in revenue yield, with various kinds of increase in income tax rates? Without expanding the discussion to cover the next ten years or so, the cumulative effects of alternative policies are not given their due weight. What level, for instance, might the annual interest charge reach after a decade of deficit financing?

No one can predict just what the Federal government's expenditures will amount to over the coming decade, but an estimated minimum may be set with a useful degree of confidence. Ordinarily the task might not seem worth while. But even minimum figures involve, for the coming years, amounts so much larger than those of recent years that important changes in taxation and in borrowing programs are clearly indicated. The possible courses open to the government depend in part on the magnitudes that must be dealt with. A sense of the proportions that are involved is therefore especially helpful at the present time. As one step in an endeavor to gain that sense of proportion, the figures in the present book have been assembled.

The expenditure totals assumed here are believed to be almost as small as they are likely to be under any circumstances, but they have not been squeezed down to a bedrock minimum, nor do they necessarily represent the present writer's judgment of what ought to be. The assumptions that underlie them are stated on pages 13 to 16 below. One is that the war ends with a British victory in 1943 or 1944. Perhaps by the time this volume appears a very different outcome will have been clearly indicated. But whether peace comes soon or late, or comes by negotiation or otherwise, the expenditures for defense seem unlikely to be much lower than stated in Table 2, barring early collapse of German power. They may turn out to be vastly greater.

The data for the later years of the decade are necessarily

much more loosely attached to reality. They present one of a number of possible patterns that might follow the peak of defense expenditures. They probably retain the character of approximations to minima, with the possible exceptions of the totals assumed for public works and relief in two or three of the years. The term "public works and relief" must be taken in a very loose sense. It is intended to cover any kind of outlay that the government may make to maintain employment and consumption or to maintain purchasing power, and this might include payments on insurance of certain business risks by the government, family allotments, repayment of forced loans or "deferred income," and so on. It might include even more general measures, such as extensive grants in aid to the state and local governments, support of the state and local bond market, and similar matters.

Federal expenditures, under the assumptions utilized here, rise from $13 billion in fiscal 1941 (the fiscal year ending June 30, 1941) to $23 billion in fiscal 1942 and $29 billion in fiscal 1943. Nondefense expenditures are assumed to be $7 billion a year in this period. Thus the defense program accounts for $6 billion in 1941, $16 billion in 1942, and $22 billion in 1943.

In fiscal 1944 a sharp decrease to $12 billion is assumed for defense spending, and a further decline to $6 billion the next year. Thereafter, defense expenditures are set at $4 billion to $5 billion a year. But nondefense expenditures are assumed to rise sharply in a hypothetical post-defense depression as a large public works and relief program is launched. Consequently, annual Federal expenditures for all purposes stay in the range $15 billion to $17 billion in the latter half of the decade.

These figures rest on an assumption that the price level will rise only moderately in the next few years and then decline moderately. What kind of program of taxing and borrowing (among other things) is necessary to insure that the price level will behave in some such manner? No direct answer is given to that question in the present book; that is a topic for further research now being carried on in several different studies, including one in which the present writer is participating. But some possible tax programs and borrowing programs are outlined here and are expressed in rough quantitative terms.

The fiscal problem over the short term, the next two years, is not the same as that over the longer term, the coming ten years or so. The most striking aspect of the short-term problem is that traditional, ordinary measures of taxation can make only a small impression on the huge deficits that now seem certain, unless extraordinary steps are taken, for fiscal 1942 and 1943. For example: if the tax system as it stands now (June, 1941) were not strengthened at all, the Federal deficit for 1942 would be $13 billion and for 1943, $17 billion. If the tax measure now before Congress were passed within a month or two, the deficit would drop only to about $11 billion for 1942 and $14 billion for 1943. The present study examines the results of five hypothetical sets of tax increases. Altogether the five sets would be producing an annual increment of $8 billion to the revenue system by the end of the decade; but, for reasons that will be made evident later in this study, they would reduce the 1942 deficit only to $9 billion and the 1943 deficit to $10 billion.

The difficulty, probably the impossibility, of holding the price level within the desired limits in the face of such deficits raises the question: What new forms, or adaptation of old forms, of taxation must be considered for use over the next two or three years? Suggestions of a general sort have been made—for example, collection of the income tax at the source, extra taxation of income with exemption for amounts saved, taxation of "value added" from extraction of raw materials through retailing. The present study, however, is designed primarily to show the quantitative aspects of various possibilities. The computation of revenue possibilities under those unfamiliar types of tax is a technical problem of too complex a nature to be handled with the resources available for this study, which has been devoted chiefly to exploring the longer-term proportions. Consequently, the task of working out in detail whatever extraordinary measures may be needed for the next year or two must be left to other research projects, including those referred to in the second paragraph preceding. The point to be emphasized here is that neither in this book nor in any other publication of which the writer is aware has an adequate fiscal program for the next year or two been worked out in enough detail to be useful for policy-making purposes. And the dangers of simply drifting are obvious.

For the longer term, the eleven years 1941–51, the basic assumptions concerning expenditures would lead to a cumulated deficit of $79 billion for that period and a public debt of $126 billion as of June 30, 1951, if the tax system as of June, 1941, were not strengthened at all; but, since there is no doubt that the tax system will be strengthened, it is more useful to consider some results under various hypothetical increases in taxation.

If income and estate taxes are increased severely in ways described below under the "first set" of tax changes,[1] the deficit for 1942 is $11 billion and for 1943, $14 billion. The cumulated deficit for the eleven years would be $50 billion, and the public debt of June 30, 1951, about $97 billion. This hypothetical "first set" of tax changes would be somewhat lighter than the program now being proposed by the

[1] See p. 26.

Treasury. The former would yield about $1.6 billion in added revenue in 1942 and $3.1 billion in 1943;[2] the Treasury program, about $2.6 billion in 1942 and $3.6 billion in 1943.

With a hypothetical "second set" of tax changes added—consisting of a further increase in the personal income tax—the total increase in taxation becomes $2.2 billion in 1942 and $4.3 billion in 1943 (by which time it takes full effect), and hence reflects a somewhat stronger taxing program than the one that is being currently debated. Even under this stronger tax program, the deficit figures are large enough to pose interesting problems of debt technique and price control. The annual deficit is then $11 billion in 1942 and $13 billion in 1943—but it is only $1 billion in 1944, and changes to a $1-billion surplus in 1945. The deficit then returns and rises to a secondary peak of $5 billion in 1947. The cumulated deficit for the eleven years, under this set of assumptions, is $39 billion, and the public debt becomes $86 billion by June 30, 1951.

The addition of a "third set" of tax changes—increases in excises—bringing in another billion dollars or so a year, cuts the cumulated deficit for the eleven years to about $28 billion, and the Federal debt on June 30, 1951, to some $75 billion. Data are also given for a "fourth set" and "fifth set" of tax measures, but they are probably not worth summarizing here, for they imply a tax structure so heavy that it might not allow the national income to rise to the levels assumed in the later years of the decade. For what it may be worth, it may be noted that with the addition of a 4 percent manufacturers' sales tax (food exempt) the cumulated deficit is only $17 billion (though the outstanding debt meanwhile rises to a peak of $70 billion in 1943); and with certain payroll tax increases piled on top of all the rest, the

[2] All years refer to fiscal year ending in year given, unless otherwise stated.

cumulated deficit is only $6 billion. This last figure, however, seems almost surely outside the realm of reality.

The sources from which the government might borrow to finance these various hypothetical deficits are examined in Chapter III. As a first approximation, it is assumed that the interest rate is kept low throughout the decade. The annual interest charge, which will be about $1.2 billion in 1942, would be $2.4 billion in 1951 if the tax system were not strengthened at all, but since it surely will be strengthened, a better figure to use for 1951 is $1.8 billion, to fit the circumstances under, say, the first set plus the second set of tax changes.[8] In other words, unless there is to be a far more drastic taxing program than the one now being debated in Congress, it appears impossible that the annual interest charge on the Federal budget will be much less than $2 billion by the end of the decade. This remark assumes that no extensive use is made of paper-money issue or an interest-free creation of deposits for government use by commercial banks.

If new borrowing from now on had to be done at a 5 percent rate (6 percent or more on fully taxable bonds) instead of the 2 percent average rate assumed here (actually, nearer 2½ percent now that all future Federal issues will be fully taxable), the annual interest charge in 1951 would be not $1.8 billion but $3.3 billion—and the cumulated deficit for the eleven years would be not $39 billion but $50 billion. (All these data assume the first two tax changes in force throughout the decade.) Obviously, the rate of interest is go-

[8] The $1.8 billion figure would actually appear as $2.0 billion or $2.1 billion in the hypothetical budget document for 1951, since the total as shown there would include, in addition to the $1.8 billion basic figure used here, $0.1 billion or so of interest on debt held by the Federal government itself (see note a to Table 2, and Appendix 2), and another $0.1 or $0.2 billion to allow for the higher interest rate occasioned by the fully taxable character of the new Federal bonds (see note 4, p. 15, and note 3, p. 76) and the dependence on Defense Savings Bonds for a large part of the financing (see p. 89).

ing to be of great concern to the Treasury, from the purely expense point of view. What sources may it tap at the low interest rates?

If no coercive drive is made to sell Federal bonds, it would appear likely that under almost any taxing policy the commercial banks will be called on to absorb large amounts of bonds in addition to those they now hold. Suppose, for instance, that, with the first two sets of tax changes in force, the cumulated deficit for the three years 1941–43 was $28 billion (see Table 13); that Savings Bonds and Defense Savings Bonds brought in $1 billion in fiscal 1941, $3 billion in 1942, and $4 billion in 1943 (an estimate that is perhaps optimistic,[4] since the heavy taxes postulated in the first two sets would cut down the bond-buying capacity); that insurance companies and mutual savings banks together absorbed $400 million in 1941, $1 billion in 1942, and $1 billion in 1943 (by which time they too would feel the effects of the tax increase); and that business corporations increased by $2 billion their holdings of government bonds over this three-year period (although many of them are selling their bonds now to get working capital, and in Table 15 no net increase at all is assumed for the eleven-year period through 1951)—then only $12.4 billion would be borrowed from sources other than the commercial banks, and the latter would have to take up nearly $16 billion in Federal bonds from July 1, 1940, to June 30, 1943, unless indeed the Federal Reserve Banks found it necessary to step in and add to their holdings, as they might have to if interest rates were to be kept low. On June 30, 1940, the commercial banks held $16.5 billion of Federal bonds. Hence it may be said that a doubling of those holdings by June 30, 1943, is by no means an improbability if the tax system is not soon strengthened far beyond the amounts indicated in the bill currently before

[4] A somewhat more conservative figure is used on p. 88 below.

Congress and if an intensive drive bordering on the compulsory is not undertaken to get individuals—and corporations?—to take up added billions of Federal debt in the coming two years.

All this is said in no alarmist spirit, for surely the situation can be kept in hand if the quantities involved are viewed realistically and a well-balanced fiscal program is developed in the course of the next few months; but surely, also, the amounts involved are large enough to make necessary a readjustment of perspective to a landscape in which the proportions have suddenly altered almost beyond recognition.

To avoid cumulative errors of some significance, the calculations have been carried through in terms of tenths of billions of dollars; but the results are generally significant only in terms of the nearest billion dollars, so uncertain are all the factors surrounding the computations.

Chapter II

ASSUMPTIONS WITH RESPECT TO EXPENDITURES

ASSUMPTIONS UNDERLYING EXPENDITURES FIGURES

THE FEDERAL expenditures for the period 1941–51 as assumed in Tables 1 and 2 are the hypothetical data on which all other figures are based. But these expenditures themselves rest on some fundamental assumptions concerning the course of the war and the post-war economy which are listed below. They have been chosen from among a great number of perhaps equally likely possibilities for two reasons. First, they are apparently (as nearly as can be judged) the assumptions on which the present policy of the United States is based—at least they are not inconsistent with that policy. Second, they tend somewhat to give a minimum rather than a maximum of total expenditures, and, from the viewpoint of research technique, a first effort in showing the quantitative relationships is easier to manage if the bias is set in that direction (but see No. 7 below). They are presented not as prophecies but as reasonable hypotheses, necessary to give real meaning to the problems and quantities involved in Federal fiscal policy. And some of the assumptions (especially Nos. 9 and 11) would not be equally reasonable under all fiscal policies.

This set of basic assumptions is:

1. That the war will end sometime in 1943 or 1944 in a British victory.

2. That the United States will send no expeditionary force.

3. That the United States armament program will continue at a high rate, the productive effort of the country in the calendar years of 1942, 1943, and part of 1944 being pushed close to the stage where unemployment will be not more than 1,000,000 or so, and where costs will be rising sharply.

4. That, starting sometime in fiscal 1944, a substantial decrease in defense expenditures will take place.

5. That such expenditures will reach a new minimum level that will be kept fairly constant during the fiscal years 1946–51.

6. That the decrease in armament expenditures will tend to bring a sharp decline in both government employment and private employment in 1944 and for two or three years thereafter. (It would be illuminating to assume instead that a post-war boom would develop and would last for two or three years; there is, however, some doubt whether the factors that produced the boom of 1919–20 would be present again in similar strength.) [1]

7. That the Federal government, after allowing the decline in employment to proceed a moderate distance, will check it by inaugurating a large public works program and will absorb most of the remaining unemployment (excluding the irreducible minimum, which the states and localities and social security will be covering) in work relief (WPA). The amounts given in Table 2, reaching a peak of $5 billion in 1947, may well prove to be too large, and are not pre-

[1] But see, for instance, the possibility of "a severe economic shock" followed by "a period of wild industrial activity" foreseen by the chairman of the employment relations committee of the National Association of Manufacturers as reported in the *Journal of Commerce* of March 4, 1941.

sented here as a necessarily desirable program to follow. To bring out the issues involved, however, it seemed best to assume that they might be large. Only in this way can the quantitative implications of a large-scale attack on a severe depression be revealed.[2]

8. That private enterprise will revive in 1947, reaching a cycle peak in 1950, but a peak that will leave unemployed in private enterprise an appreciable number of employables.

9. That the wholesale commodity price index of the Bureau of Labor Statistics will rise only moderately from calendar 1941 to calendar 1943, then decline by 1946 to slightly below the calendar 1939 level, and then rise slightly in calendar 1948; and that the cost-of-living index of the Bureau will fluctuate within a fairly narrow range throughout the ten years (see Table 3). Probably this assumption can be valid only under one kind of tax and debt policy. Unfortunately, there is as yet little agreement on just which policy would fit this description. Some of the more extreme policies illustrated in the following pages would almost surely not fit. If, for instance, the tax system were not strengthened at all, prices would presumably rise much more than is assumed here. But the extreme illustrations are presented nevertheless, as being helpful in giving a sense of proportion.[3]

10. That no important changes will occur during the next ten years in the scope or intensity of expenditures for

  a. The ordinary administrative expenses of government
  b. Veterans' pensions and benefits

[2] Cf. the recent announcement by Federal Works Administrator John M. Carmody that a series of conferences will be held with the newly organized Public Works Reserve to discuss plans for the expenditure of from $25 billion to $30 billion over six years in the post-defense period. *Journal of Commerce*, July 7, 1941.

[3] See p. vi, Preface, above. Indeed, as the book goes to press, wholesale prices and the cost of living already show signs of exceeding, in 1941, the levels assumed in Table 3.

c. Aids to agriculture

d. Aids to youth

e. Social Security administrative expenses and grants to states for assistance programs

These assumptions, again, are not intended to imply anything concerning the desirability of cutting, not cutting, or increasing the nondefense expenditures. The fact is that powerful pressures are being exerted in both directions, and the assumptions used here simply steer a middle course for purposes of illustration.

11. That a low-interest policy will be followed, successfully, throughout the decade, so that the average rate on new Federal obligations will be equivalent to about 2 percent for bonds exempt from the corporation normal tax—that is, an actual interest rate on the new, taxable issues nearer 2½ percent.[4] This assumption, like Number 9, depends to some extent on the assumptions with respect to volume and type of borrowing and taxation.

12. That the old-age benefit payments will increase in accordance with the estimate made in the Senate Finance Committee report on the Social Security Amendments of 1939.

On the basis of this series of assumptions it is further assumed that the figure for national income produced will rise to a yearly peak of $100 billion in calendar 1943, fall to $75 billion in calendar 1946 and rise to $90 billion in calendar 1949 and 1950 (see Table 3). Comparisons with other estimates of national income, published and unpub-

[4] The rate is computed on a tax-free basis for the present study because the tax-revenue estimates of the Treasury for hypothetical high-income years (see page 22 below) were evidently computed on this basis, being made before the enactment of the Public Debt Act of 1941. Although the additional interest charge that will have to be met because of the removal of tax exemption will not be exactly counterbalanced by the income tax revenues resulting from this measure, the difference will probably not be significant in terms of tenths of billions.

lished, indicate that those presented here tend more to an underestimate than to an overestimate; but, on the other hand, no radical change—for example, to $110 billion or $120 billion as a maximum—seems justifiable unless our assumptions about the price level are changed. The $75-billion and $80-billion figures for 1946 and 1947 may be considered somewhat low in view of the assumption that the government will intervene to absorb most of the idle man power through public works and WPA. Again, the validity of the income figures depends largely on the kinds and extent of taxation and of borrowing by which these expenditures are financed. The income figures as used here are meant simply to imply that the depression might be as deep as that of, say, 1937–39, or even more so, in terms of private enterprise, were it not for the large-scale public works program assumed here, and that, in terms of giving men some kind of employment (if only WPA), the situation would not be allowed to deteriorate much below the 1940 level.

EXPENDITURES RESULTING FROM THE UNDERLYING ASSUMPTIONS

On the basis of the assumptions above, the expenditures of the Federal government from fiscal 1941 to 1951 inclusive are set down in Table 1. (The term "estimated," even with all the qualifications that the assumptions imply, would carry too strong a connotation of dependability for the present case.) These expenditures represent the total outlays passing from the government into private hands, with some exceptions that are not important for purposes of this study. Only the net results of the postal service, for instance, are shown, and the interest payments on the guaranteed debt are not included, since they are met largely by revenues of the corporations in question.[5] The figures for defense expenditure in-

[5] See Appendix 2.

Table 1

Federal Expenditures (National Defense and Other) for Fiscal 1941–51 under the Assumptions Given on Pages 13–16

(In Billions of Dollars. Derived from Table 2)

	1941	*1942*	*1943*	*1944*	*1945*	*1946*	*1947*	*1948*	*1949*	*1950*	*1951*
National defense including lease-lend to Britain and others	6.0	16	22	12	6	4	4	4	5	5	5
All other expenditures	6.6	7	7	7	10	12	13	13	10	11	10
Total	12.6	23	29	19	16	16	17	17	15	16	15

clude whatever expenditure program might be carried out in the name of the RFC or other similar government corporation.[6] The figures include aid to Great Britain and other anti-Axis powers. They do not include appropriations to the old-age reserve account, since the expenditures for future years include the outpayments from this reserve. This treatment has not been attempted for the smaller Federal trust accounts (as in the *Daily Treasury Statement*); for these accounts, the expenditure totals reflect the amounts going into the reserves instead of the payments from the reserves.

The expenditure figures are given in somewhat more detail in Table 2.

The total rises from $13 billion in 1941 to $23 billion in 1942 and $29 billion in 1943, dropping to $16 billion in 1945 and fluctuating between $15 billion and $17 billion through 1951. These totals are probably too low. The only items in which there seems to have been a chance for important errors of overestimate are (1) the national defense expenditures for 1943; (2) the work relief expenditures (WPA and PWA) of $19 billion for the five years 1945–49 inclusive (see assumptions Nos. 6 and 7 above), and (3) the interest charge. This last item is overestimated because, as a first step in the analysis, the deficits have been computed under the assumption that the tax system as it stood at the end of May, 1941, would not be strengthened at all during the decade. Actually, of course, it will be strengthened. Subsequent steps in the computation will take account of the saving in interest that would occur as the deficits were lessened by increases in taxation. On the other hand, chances for underestimate result from the assumptions that the price

[6] Defense expenditures by RFC and other government corporations are especially difficult to estimate, in view of some dangers of double counting. A few tenths of a billion should probably be allocated to 1941 on this account, but in the absence of definite information, a lump-sum allowance of $1 billion has been made specifically for 1942 (see note g, Table 2).

Table 2

FEDERAL EXPENDITURES (FIVE MAJOR CATEGORIES) FOR FISCAL 1941–51 UNDER THE ASSUMPTIONS GIVEN ON PAGES 13–16

(In Billions of Dollars)

	1941[b]	1942[f]	1943	1944	1945	1946	1947	1948	1949	1950	1951
National defense, including aid to Britain and others	6.0[c]	16.5[g]	22.0	12.0	6	4	4	4	5	5	5
Work relief and public works (WPA, PWA)	1.4	0.9	0.6	0.6	3	4	5	5	2	2	1
Interest[a]	1.0[d]	1.2[h]	1.5	1.7	2	2	2	2	2	3	3
All other expenditures	4.2[e]	4.5	4.5	4.9	5	6	6	6	6	6	6
TOTAL	12.6	23.1[i]	28.6	19.2	16	16	17	17	15	16	15

[a] The interest item for 1942–51 is an overstatement: it is based on the deficits that might occur if no additional taxes were imposed. This assumption is necessary simply as a first step in the analysis. The interest item does not include interest on the guaranteed debt (see p. 109).

[b] *Daily Treasury Statement* of June 30, 1941.

[c] Almost, but not precisely, comparable with the classification used by the Budget Bureau and reflected in the 1942 figure. The difference is apparently about $0.2 billion for 1941.

[d] Reduced by $0.1 billion from the *Daily Treasury Statement* figure, to eliminate interest on special issues held by Old Age Fund (see Appendix 2).

[e] After deduction of $0.3 billion representing return of surplus funds of government corporations.

[f] From *Statement* of June 1, 1941, by Director of Bureau of Budget, except as otherwise noted.

[g] The *Statement* figure of $15.5 billion, plus $1.0 billion as a rough estimate of defense expenditures by RFC and other government corporations.

[h] Reduced by $0.1 billion from estimate in the *Statement;* see note d above.

[i] The total in the *Statement* is $22.2 billion.

level will remain fairly stable, that the rearming program will be virtually completed by 1945, that aids to agriculture, youth, the aged, and veterans will not rise substantially (old-age benefit payments excepted), that other forms of social security will not absorb important amounts of money, and that interest rates will remain low—to say nothing of the basic assumption that the United States will not make active use of its army in the war. Moreover, some of the estimates, or rather goals, set by official bodies other than the Treasury give defense expenditures for fiscal 1942 that run from $5 billion to $10 billion above the $15.5 Budget Bureau estimate.[7]

National Income, et Cetera, Consistent with the Underlying Assumptions.—In developing the assumptions about the background of business activity, which were helpful in suggesting assumptions concerning expenditures and receipts, wholesale-price index figures were first set down. These figures imply that costs will increase appreciably as less efficient labor and capital goods are drawn in by the intense effort to increase production, but they also imply that hourly wage rates, regular and overtime, will not be raised appreciably from present levels and that consumers, in one way or another, will be prevented from bidding up prices well above costs (as will be noted below, this implication carries some further implications concerning the taxation and borrowing policies). The cost-of-living index was then assumed, on the basis of recent experience, to be consistent with the wholesale index. Then national income figures were chosen that seemed to be consistent with these price assumptions and with the basic assumptions concerning the intensity of the booms and the intervening depression and the times at which they would occur. The resulting figures are shown in Table 3.

[7] Office for Emergency Management, *Defense—One Year,* chart on p. 30.

TABLE 3

PRICE INDEXES AND NATIONAL INCOME POSTULATED UNDER THE ASSUMPTIONS GIVEN ON PAGES 13–16; CALENDAR 1940–50

	1940	*1941*	*1942*	*1943*	*1944*	*1945*	*1946*	*1947*	*1948*	*1949*	*1950*
Wholesale prices (Bureau of Labor Statistics index)	79 [a]	84	87	90	85	80	75	75	80	80	80
Cost of living (Bureau of Labor Statistics index)	100 [b]	102	105	108	106	102	98	98	100	100	100
National income produced (in billions)	$76 [c]	$84 [d]	$90	$100	$90	$80	$75	$80	$85	$90	$90

[a] *Federal Reserve Bulletin*, March, 1941, p. 254.
[b] *Survey of Current Business*, May, 1941, p. 18.
[c] *Ibid.*, June, 1941.
[d] As this book goes to press, it appears that this estimate is low. The *Federal Reserve Bulletin* for August, 1941, p. 724, notes that "national income payments by June had advanced to a rate of about $88,000,000,000 a year. . . ."

REVENUES FROM PRESENT SYSTEM, RESULTING FROM UNDERLYING ASSUMPTIONS

As a first step in the computations, there is presented, in Table 4, the yield of the Federal revenue system that might be produced if the rates and other provisions of the tax laws existing in May, 1941, remain unchanged, with the national income totals as given in Table 3. The revenue rises from $8.3 billion in fiscal 1941 to $12.7 billion in fiscal 1944, then declines to $9.0 billion in fiscal 1947, and rises to $11.7 billion in fiscal 1951. The 1941 figures are from the *Daily Treasury Statement* of June 30, 1941. For 1943 and later years, the figures are based on the estimates, submitted on page 5 of the 1940 report of the Secretary of the Treasury, of the yield of the present tax system under a national income of $90 billion and $100 billion. Allowance is made for the lag in collections under the income taxes and the estate tax. The income tax group is the only one in Table 4 that shows a variation large enough to be significant in the present discussion. It increases from $3.5 billion in 1941 to $7.7 billion in 1944. Part of this increase reflects the increased rates and lowered exemptions enacted in 1940 and the introduction of the excess profits tax the same year.[8] Similarly, part of the increase in "other taxes" (from $3.0 billion in 1941 to $3.4 billion in 1944) reflects increased rates enacted in the (First) Revenue Act of 1940.

In view of the extent to which tax revenues even for fiscal 1941 have exceeded the expectations as stated in the Budget for 1942, the Treasury's estimates of the yield at higher income levels may prove somewhat conservative, though it ap-

[8] In principle, some allowance is called for on account of the "relief" provisions for taxpayers under the excess profits tax, passed early in 1941, but the amount appears to be uncertain and too small, relative to the total revenue of the Federal tax system, to warrant an adjustment in the present figures.

TABLE 4

FEDERAL REVENUES FOR FISCAL 1941–51 UNDER THE REVENUE ACTS OF 1940 AND THE ASSUMPTIONS GIVEN ON PAGES 13–16

(In Billions of Dollars)

	1941[a]	1942[b]	1943	1944	1945	1946	1947	1948	1949	1950	1951
Income taxes (individual income, corporation income, excess profits, declared value excess profits, unjust enrichment)	3.5	5.4	6.6	7.7	7.4	5.8	4.7	4.5	5.6	6.2	6.6
Employment taxes (old-age payroll taxes, including railroads, and Federal share of unemployment insurance taxes, including railroads)	0.9	[c]	1.0	1.1	1.0	1.0	0.9	1.0	1.0	1.1	1.1
Customs	0.4	0.4	0.3	0.3	0.3	0.3	0.3	0.3	0.3	0.3	0.3
Other taxes (chiefly on estates, liquor, tobacco, gasoline, and capital stock)	3.0	[c]	3.2	3.4	3.3	3.1	2.9	3.1	3.2	3.4	3.5
Miscellaneous revenues	0.2	0.2	0.2	0.2	0.2	0.2	0.2	0.2	0.2	0.2	0.2
Return of surplus funds from Government corporations	0.3	..	..	..	..	..	..	..	..	..	..
TOTAL	8.3	10.1	11.3	12.7	12.2	10.4	9.0	9.1	10.3	11.2	11.7

[a] *Daily Treasury Statement* of June 30, 1941.
[b] From *Statement* of June 1, 1941, by Director of Bureau of Budget.
[c] Details not available.

pears that the recent favorable showing has in part been due to a more rapid rise in national income than was anticipated and hence only in part to a change in the anticipated relation of tax revenues to national income.

The term "revenues," as used here, means tax revenues, "miscellaneous revenues" (fees, etc., of $0.2 billion a year), and a part of the "return of surplus funds of government corporations" in 1941 (the rest is accounted for as a subtraction from expenditures).

HYPOTHETICAL DEFICITS RESULTING FROM UNDERLYING ASSUMPTIONS IF NO STRENGTHENING OF TAX SYSTEM

Still merely as a first step in the computations, there may be computed the excess of the outlays in Table 2 over the revenues in Table 4. These revenues, it will be recalled, are certainly smaller than those that will in fact be collected (and the deficits consequently are too large), since the tax system will certainly be strengthened. Moreover, if the deficits were indeed to be of this size, the price level and the national income assumed in Table 3 would presumably be too low. Consequently the deficits computed in this manner are useful only for giving a sense of the size of the fiscal problem that now faces the country. They cumulate to $79 billion for the eleven-year period 1941–51. The annual deficit figure rises from $4.3 billion in 1941 to $13 billion in 1942, then increases to $17 billion in 1943, and drops to $7 billion in 1944 and $4 billion in 1945 (all figures are for fiscal years ending in the year stated). It then rises, owing to the assumed depression, to $6 billion in 1946 and $8 billion in 1947 and 1948, and it drops thereafter to $5 billion in 1949, $5 billion in 1950, and $3 billion in 1951. Again it must be emphasized that these deficits are only first steps in a study of what may happen; on the one hand, the tax system will surely be strengthened, and, on the other hand, if it were not, deficits of this magnitude would likely lead to a substantial rise in the price level which would in turn affect the size of the deficits themselves.

Chapter III

TAXATION

Various ways are open to decrease the deficits computed in the preceding paragraph through strengthening the tax system. Among the many possibilities, five changes or sets of changes are considered here. The first set consists of a sharp increase in personal income tax rates, a more moderate rise in the corporation income tax, a very sharp increase in the rates of the estate and gift taxes, and some changes in the statutory definition of net income and net estate. The second change consists of a further increase in personal income tax rates. The third is a set of increases in the taxes on liquor, cigarettes, gasoline, and automobiles. The fourth is a manufacturers' sales tax. The fifth assumes (as Table 4 did not) that the old-age payroll taxes will increase in accordance with the time schedule now in the law. No particular importance should be attached to the order of these changes. The order was selected partly with a view to what seems most likely to occur in the near future (it has been evident for some time that the personal income tax would be strengthened before serious consideration would be given to a manufacturers' sales tax), and partly because it seemed advisable to complete the more difficult tasks of estimating (for example, the increases in the personal income tax) before going further. The order does not strictly represent the views of the present writer with respect to the relative desirability of these measures; for example, the scheduled increases in the payroll taxes may well be considered to rank ahead of any of the others in desirability, if only because of the commitments that have been made under the old-age benefit program. Omissions have been dictated in part by the difficulty of making estimates, as is the case to some extent with a lowering of the income tax exemptions. There is, then, no effort here to compare carefully the merits of the alternatives open to Congress.[1]

With respect to the period following 1944, each of the various assumptions given here concerning tax changes is open to the serious objection that, once made, the assumption is carried straight through to the end of 1951 without change. Actually, some of the tax increases enacted for the period of prosperity may well be repealed when depression supervenes—at least, this is likely to be the fact, whatever the advantages or disadvantages of such action might be. To try to vary each of the several tax patterns with the phases of business activity would complicate the picture too much for the purposes of this brief survey; but the corresponding limitation to the validity of the revenue data for the assumed post-defense period needs to be kept in mind.

INCREASING TAX REVENUE UNDER THE FIRST SET OF TAX CHANGES

Income Tax (Individual).—An increased revenue could be obtained from the individual income tax by raising the present normal tax rate of 4.4 percent. However, the same increase could be obtained by starting the surtax rates at a lower level, and by increasing them at existing levels. The surtax rates now apply only to the net income after deduction of personal exemption and credit for dependents and

[1] For a treatment of some of the chief issues involved, the reader is referred to the present writer's article, "Choice of Tax Measures to Avert Inflation," *Review of Economic Statistics*, May, 1941, pp. 88–90.

after a further exemption of $4,000. The interest on virtually all Federal bonds now outstanding is exempt from the normal tax; much of it, on the other hand, is subject to the surtax. Moreover, the credit for earned income applies only for the normal tax, not the surtax. For these two reasons, a given percent additional rate yields more revenue when it takes the form of surtax rather than normal tax.

The data on calendar year 1937 individual income (the latest for which full information has been published) are grouped in *Statistics of Income* (Table 2, p. 117) according to the size of the taxpayer's net income. They tell us, for instance, that there were 1,318,340 taxable returns that showed a net income of $1,000 or more, but less than $2,000; that this particular group of returns showed an aggregate net income of $1,948,933,783—and so on; or, to go farther up the scale, there were 45,967 returns that showed a net income of $15,000 or more but less than $20,000, with an aggregate net income of $791,103,344—and so on. They do not, however, show us how much of the income from all these taxpayers, rich and poor, falls between each of the various income levels —how much, for instance, of the $791,103,344 falls in the zero to $4,000 range, where the surtax rates do not apply; how much of it falls in the $4,000 to $6,000 range, where the surtax rate is 4.4 percent; how much in the $6,000 to $8,000 range, where the rate is 6.6 percent—and so on. This information is needed before an estimate can be made of the amount of revenue that might come from increasing those surtax rates—for example, increasing the 4.4 percent to, say, 10 percent, or the 6.6 percent to 13 percent. This kind of information, although not supplied directly in the *Statistics of Income*, can be derived from the data therein. The results are shown in Table 5. The 1937 data have been adjusted to take account of the lowering of the personal exemptions, under the Revenue Act of 1940, from $1,000 to $800 (single

Table 5

AMOUNT OF 1937 SURTAX NET INCOME IN EACH SURTAX INCOME RANGE

Range or Bracket of Surtax Net Income (Net Income Minus Personal Exemption and Credit for Dependents) (Dollars)	*Aggregate Amount of Taxable Surtax Net Income (i.e., after Deducting $800 for Single and $2,000 for Married Taxpayers and Credit for Dependents) Reported by All Individuals (Including Estates and Trusts) as Received in 1937 (Millions of Dollars)*	*Yield of Hypothetical Rate Scale in Table 6 (Millions of Dollars)*
2,000 (0– 2,000)	4,370	437
2,000 (2,000– 4,000)	1,259	163
2,000 (4,000– 6,000)	769	123
2,000 (6,000– 8,000)	527	105
2,000 (8,000– 10,000)	398	96
2,000 (10,000– 12,000)	312	87
2,000 (12,000– 14,000)	252	81
2,000 (14,000– 16,000)	206	74
2,000 (16,000– 18,000)	160	64
2,000 (18,000– 20,000)	160	70
2,000 (20,000– 22,000)	118	56
4,000 (22,000– 26,000)	199	104
6,000 (26,000– 32,000)	242	136
6,000 (32,000– 38,000)	154	92
6,000 (38,000– 44,000)	147	88
6,000 (44,000– 50,000)	99	60
10,000 (50,000– 60,000)	121	74
10,000 (60,000– 70,000)	100	62
10,000 (70,000– 80,000)	70	43
10,000 (80,000– 90,000)	51	32
10,000 (90,000– 100,000)	42	26
50,000 (100,000– 150,000)	134	86
Above 150,000	299	198
TOTAL	10,192 [a]	2,357

[a] Discrepancy between total of constituent items (10,189) and true total (10,192) arises from evening off to nearest million and from certain short cuts in technique.

persons) and from $2,500 to $2,000 (married couples and heads of families). This adjustment has been made only with respect to those who reported taxable income in 1937; the question of new taxpayers uncovered by this lowering is considered on page 33.

The data in Table 5 do not mean, for instance, that the group of taxpayers that had a surtax net income of $38,000 to $44,000 showed an aggregate net income of $147 million. They mean, instead, that all the taxpayers together who have a surtax net income of more than $38,000—including those whose surtax net incomes were $50,000, $100,000, and so on—had $147 million of that income falling in the range or bracket of from $38,000 to $44,000. Thus a $50,000 surtax net income would have $6,000 falling in that bracket ($44,000 minus $38,000); so would a $100,000 income. A $41,000 income would have only $3,000 falling there. A $37,000 income would have none falling there.

Well over half the total surtax net income under the 1937 taxable returns fell in the zero to $4,000 bracket, where the surtax rate at present is zero. About one eighth fell in the $4,000 to $8,000 range, where the rates are 4.4 percent ($4,000 to $6,000) and 6.6 percent ($6,000 to $8,000).

The present surtax rate scale, that is, the scale prescribed by the Revenue Act of 1940, when applied to the income shown in Table 5, gives $1.1 billion in tax. A hypothetical surtax rate scale, embodying the increase in rates that is to be assumed under the first set of tax changes, is drawn up in Table 6, and this scale is then applied to the data in Table 5 to get an estimate of yield on the 1937 situation. This hypothetical surtax scale has no official or semiofficial basis; it simply represents an increase that, although severe, seems not beyond the bounds of immediate consideration.[2] For

[2] This scale was drawn up before the Treasury presented its proposal late in April, 1941, and is somewhat more severe than the latter for incomes

purposes of comparison, Table 6 also shows the present surtax scale (the present scale includes a 10 percent addition on account of the defense tax, though the defense tax is not formally a part of the "surtax" rate structure).

This hypothetical scale contains an anomaly in that it does not allow the deduction for earned income that is allowed for the normal tax. Hence, an individual might be taxable under the surtax but not the normal tax. It might be preferable to reduce the earned income credit and allow it against both normal tax and surtax.

The hypothetical scale shows no increase over present surtax rates for brackets over $150,000. This merely reflects the fact that, whatever the economic or equitable aspects of an increase above that level, the amount of revenue that would be obtained would not be large enough to be significant for the present discussion. Out of the $299 million in surtax net income falling in brackets above that level (1937 data), the present surtax rates take about $200 million (note that this does not say that taxpayers with surtax net incomes of more than $150,000 have $299 million in surtax net income, and so on). The taxpayers with surtax net incomes of more than $150,000 would nevertheless pay an increased tax under the hypothetical surtax rate scale; the higher rates in the lower brackets of income would affect them. The increased burden would come out of the bottom of their incomes, so to speak, not out of the top.

The rates in the hypothetical surtax scale are applied to the amounts of income shown in Table 5, and the results are given in the right-hand column of that table. The total surtax yield is roughly $2.4 billion. This is an increase of $1.3 billion over the yield obtained by applying the present surtax rates to the income in Table 5.

above $20,000 or so, and somewhat lighter on lower incomes. See Table 7 below.

Table 6

HYPOTHETICAL AND PRESENT SURTAX RATE SCALES

(Each Rate Is Applicable Only to Corresponding Bracket of Income, Not to Taxpayer's Entire Income)

Range, or Bracket, of Surtax Net Income (Net Income after Deducting Personal Exemption and Credit for Dependents)	*Hypothetical Scale (Percent)*	*Present Surtax Scale (Including 10 Percent Increase Due to Defense Tax)*
$ 0–$ 2,000	10	0
2,000– 4,000	13	0
4,000– 6,000	16	4.4
6,000– 8,000	20	6.6
8,000– 10,000	24	8.8
10,000– 12,000	28	11.0
12,000– 14,000	32	13.2
14,000– 16,000	36	16.5
16,000– 18,000	40	19.8
18,000– 20,000	44	23.1
20,000– 22,000	48	26.4
22,000– 26,000	52	29.7
26,000– 32,000	56	33
32,000– 38,000	60	36.3
38,000– 44,000	60	39.6
44,000– 50,000	61	44
50,000– 60,000	61	48.4
60,000– 70,000	62	51.7
70,000– 80,000	62	55
80,000– 90,000	63	58.5
90,000– 100,000	63	61.6
100,000– 150,000	64	63.8 [a]
Above 150,000	Same as at present	68 [a] to 76.7 [a]

[a] Approximate. The law reads that the amount added by the defense tax—that is, normally, 10 percent of the *tax* (not the income) otherwise due—shall not exceed 10 percent of the amount by which the net income exceeds the tax computed without regard to the defense tax. Thus the maximum average rate of normal tax plus surtax plus defense tax cannot exceed 75 plus 4 plus 10 percent of 21, or 81.1 percent. If 0.4 percent be allotted as increase in normal tax, the top rate on the surtax thus becomes 76.7. For the same reason the figure of 68 is approximate; and the figure of 63.8 is not strictly applicable through the whole range $100,000–$150,000.

The individual income tax (surtax and normal tax) may yield, under present rates, nearly $2.0 billion in fiscal 1942.[3] This may be compared with what the present rates, surtax and normal tax, would produce on the 1937 incomes; and this is roughly $1.5 billion.[4] Hence fiscal 1942, making a better showing than calendar 1937 on the basis of the present rate scale, could be expected to make a better showing than calendar 1937 under a higher rate scale also. Possibly the increase of $1.3 billion noted above could be raised to about $1.7 billion.[5]

These estimates do not take account of those who are brought within the individual income tax by the lowering of the exemptions (Revenue Act of 1940) to $800 and $2,000. *Statistics of Income* contains no data that can indicate even a rough answer on this point. But, judging from the very small amount of revenue that the Treasury expects from these new taxpayers,[6] the increased tax which they would pay under the hypothetical surtax schedule would be negligible for the purposes of the present discussion.

[3] As judged from the Budget for 1942 and the revisions (not presented, however, in much detail) in the *Statement* of June 1, 1941, by the Director of the Bureau of the Budget.

[4] Surtax, $1.1 billion as above; normal tax: actually collected, as shown by *Statistics of Income,* at 4 percent rate, $335 million; add 10 percent for defense tax, $34 million; total, $1.5 billion.

[5] This $1.7 billion includes an estimated $100 million allowed because of certain technical considerations, including two technical biases inherent in the method used for distributing the income among the brackets.

[6] The amount is $14 million. Senate Finance Committee, *Report No. 1856,* June 15, 1940, pp. 9–10. In testimony before the Senate Finance Committee on the Revenue Act of 1941, August 8, 1941, Assistant Secretary of the Treasury John L. Sullivan is reported to have estimated that a decrease of the $2,000 exemption to $1,500 and of the $800 exemption to $750 would add $303 million revenue under the new high rate scale under consideration, by far the largest part coming from those who would pay a tax even if the exemptions were unchanged. The number of taxpayers under the $2,000 and $800 exemptions (with the surtax rate applying immediately above those levels, with no earned income credit against it) would be 10,925,000; under the $1,500 and $750 exemptions it would rise to 13,200,000 (23,650,000

To the increase of $1.7 billion for a full fiscal year 1942 there may be added something that could come from certain other adjustments. A stricter policy with respect to some of the deductions in computing net income is possible: for instance, with respect to depletion allowances and certain nonbusiness deductions. Long-term capital gains could be taxed more heavily (at present, gains from the sale of assets held over two years are taxed at a maximum rate of 16.5 percent, no matter how wealthy the taxpayer). These measures might add between $100 million and $200 million a year. Interest on issues of state and local obligations might be made subject to the Federal income tax. There is a considerable body of opinion among students of constitutional law that such taxation would be upheld by the Supreme Court. If the tax were confined to interest on future issues, the added revenue from this source would be far below $100 million a year for the rest of the decade or even longer. If the interest on all outstanding state and local issues were made taxable, the increase in revenue would approach but probably not surpass $100 million annually at once. It has been estimated that individuals held $7.9 billion of state and local securities on June 30, 1940.[7] If the average coupon rate were 3½ percent, the gross tax base (including nontaxable persons) for individuals would increase by some $280 million. Active banks (except mutual savings banks) held $3.6 billion, and ordinary corporations $0.5 billion.[8] Hence the gross tax base for corporations might be increased by some $140 million. Some deductible capital losses would be

would have to file returns, on 10,450,000 of which no tax would be due owing to deductions, etc.). *New York Herald Tribune*, Aug. 9, 1941.

[7] Treasury *Bulletin*, Feb., 1941, p. 1.

[8] *Ibid.* Insurance companies held $2.1 billion. The rest were held by tax-exempt institutions or in government funds. Under the present technique of taxing insurance companies, it appears that the added revenue to come from them would be slight.

taken as the bonds fell in value. Even without assuming taxation of outstanding state and local securities, a lump sum addition of $200 million a year may be set down as coming from adjustments to the income tax if the rates have already been raised as indicated above. Hence a total of $1.9 billion increased annual revenue for a full fiscal year 1942 is reached so far as the individual income tax is concerned. For the actual fiscal 1942, only about $1.1 billion should be allowed; owing to the privilege of installment payments, fiscal 1942 collections reflect in part the taxable income of 1940, to which these increased rates would presumably not be applied. For fiscal 1943 and 1944 the added revenue is set at $2.1 billion and $2.3 billion, respectively (Table 10). These amounts are somewhat on the conservative side, to allow for the fact that any increase in the corporation net income tax (see pages 37–40) will reduce dividend payments, which for the most part go to taxpayers with large incomes.

If the hypothetical surtax rate scale in Table 6 appears unduly high, it may be noted that the average rate on the entire net income (that is, before deduction of the personal exemption and credit for dependents) is appreciably less than the bracket rates shown in that table. Thus, under the hypothetical rate scale shown in Table 6, and assuming a 4.4 percent normal tax, a married man with two dependents would pay, on a net income of $3,000, only $20 tax (2/3 of 1 percent of the net income) computed as follows:

Net income		$3,000
Personal exemption	2,000	
Credit for dependents	800	2,800
Surtax net income		200
Surtax at hypothetical (Table 6) 10 percent rate		20
Earned income allowance—subtract from surtax net income		300
Normal tax net income		None

The same taxpayer, with an earned income of $5,000, would pay a tax of $300.80—6 percent of his income:

Net income		$5,000
Personal exemption	2,000	
Credit for dependents	800	2,800
Surtax net income		2,200
Surtax under hypothetical (Table 6) rates:		
First 2,000—10 percent—200		
Next 200—13 percent— 26		
Total surtax		226
Earned income credit (10 percent of $5,000)		500
Normal tax net income		1,700
Normal tax (4.4 percent)		74.80
Total tax		300.80

The point of these illustrations is that, with the current personal exemptions, the income tax on moderate incomes will not reach what might generally be considered a very burdensome level until the surtax rates, in the lower ranges, are put up to heights that superficially might appear impracticable—for instance, an initial rate of 20 percent, instead of the 10 percent postulated in Table 6.

At somewhat higher levels the average tax rate increases sharply under the hypothetical scale. The married taxpayer with two dependents, with an income of $20,000 (and assuming the maximum earned income credit) would pay a normal tax plus hypothetical surtax of $4,755.20, or roughly 24 percent of his income.

All of these percentages would be appreciably higher for taxpayers with fewer dependents, especially single taxpayers. Table 7 gives the hypothetical tax for the intermediate case, the married couple with no dependents. The tax that would be due under some of the recent proposals and that due under the existing law (June, 1941) are also shown.

Income Tax (Corporations).—Another source of revenue that has been commonly considered is the income tax on corporations. Whether any further increase in the present top rate of 24 percent is advisable is at least doubtful. In so far as the tax is not shifted to consumers or others, it reduces the stockholders' equity in the corporations, and some of the stockholders are persons with very modest incomes. In so far as the tax is shifted, the burden is distributed erratically or at least in a little-known manner. On the other hand, fur-

TABLE 7

FEDERAL INCOME TAX FOR MARRIED COUPLE WITH NO DEPENDENTS: EXISTING LAW, HYPOTHETICAL RATE (TABLE 6 RATES PLUS EXISTING NORMAL TAX), AND CERTAIN RECENTLY PROPOSED RATES

Net Income before Personal Exemption	*Law as of June, 1941*	*Hypothetical Rate (Table 6 Surtax Rates Plus 4.4 Percent Normal Rate)* [b]	*Proposal Submitted by Treasury April, 1941* [a]	*Proposal Submitted by Joint Committee Staff April, 1941* [a]	*Proposal Submitted by Eccles April, 1941* [a]
$ 2,500	$ 11	$ 61	$ 72	$ 44	$ 70
3,000	31	100	152	97	118
4,000	70	270	312	202	234
5,000	110	440	506	352	370
6,000	150	610	700	502	526
8,000	317	1,009	1,131	889	898
10,000	528	1,488	1,628	1,364	1,345
12,500	858	2,207	2,316	2,013	1,990
15,000	1,258	3,050	3,073	2,853	2,729
20,000	2,336	5,110	4,800	4,756	4,429
25,000	3,843	7,690	6,824	7,055	6,394
50,000	14,128	22,230	19,540	20,794	19,234
75,000	27,768	38,798	35,127	36,689	35,184
100,000	43,476	55,490	52,474	54,124	52,639
500,000	330,156	341,380	346,122	347,598	354,049
1,000,000	717,584	728,800	738,086	739,598	744,034
5,000,000	3,916,548	3,927,760	3,937,050	3,938,598	3,934,004

[a] Hearings before the Committee on Ways and Means, *Revenue Revision of 1941*, p. 687.

[b] Assuming maximum earned income credit throughout.

ther taxation of corporations has been urged on the grounds that they do serve, whether designedly or incidentally, as reservoirs in which the net profits can be retained without their having to pass at once through the surtax brackets of the individual's income tax (the stockholder does not include in his personal return his share of the undistributed profits of the corporation). To what extent the tax would exercise an anti-inflationary influence by checking consumption is a complex subject requiring much more study than it has yet received. Regardless of whether the net result is advantageous or otherwise, data will be presented here, for illustrative purposes, on an increase in the 24 percent rate to 30 percent, and a similar rise of 6 percentage points on the corporations with net incomes of less than $38,565.90 (they now pay at average rates ranging from 14.85 percent to 24 percent). It was estimated about a year ago that an added 1 percent would increase the annual revenue by about $70 million, and under the higher levels of business now obtaining this might well be above $100 million.[9] If 6 percent were added all along the line, raising the rates to 20.85 to 30 percent, something between $400 million and $500 million might be expected in a full year; about half that, for the fiscal year 1942, if the change applied to calendar 1941 incomes; and as much as $500 million or $600 million under the extremely high levels of business activity that would be reflected in fiscal 1943 and 1944.[10]

[9] Assistant Secretary of the Treasury John L. Sullivan, in Senate Finance Committee, *Hearings, Revenue Act of 1940,* p. 36.

[10] See the recent Treasury estimate that $534 million would be produced in the first full year of application of an increase in the corporate rate by 5 percentage points on the first $25,000 of net income and 6 percentage points on the balance, this increase taking the form of a "surtax" and applying to the interest on those Federal bonds that are exempt from Federal "normal" taxes. Sullivan, Statement of April 24, 1941.

Adding the individual income tax figures above to these corporation estimates gives an increase of about $1.4 billion for fiscal 1942 (assuming the increases are first applicable

TABLE 8

AMOUNT OF TAXABLE NET ESTATE IN EACH ESTATE RANGE
RETURNS FILED IN 1938

Range, or Bracket, of Taxable Net Estate (Gross Estate Minus All Deductions and Minus an Exemption of $40,000 [in Some Cases $50,000]) (Dollars)	*Aggregate Amount of Taxable Net Estate Shown on Returns Filed in Calendar 1938 (Millions of Dollars)*
0– 10,000	120
10,000– 20,000	97
20,000– 30,000	82
30,000– 40,000	61
40,000– 50,000	61
50,000– 70,000	94
70,000– 100,000	113
100,000– 200,000	229
200,000– 400,000	214
400,000– 600,000	121
600,000– 800,000	78
800,000– 1,000,000	59
1,000,000– 1,500,000	98
1,500,000– 2,000,000	58
2,000,000– 2,500,000	34
2,500,000– 3,000,000	30
3,000,000– 3,500,000	24
3,500,000– 4,000,000	18
4,000,000– 4,500,000	17
4,500,000– 7,000,000	51
7,000,000–10,000,000	25
Over 10,000,000	45
TOTAL	1,725 [a]

[a] Discrepancy between total of constituent items (1,729) and true total (1,725) arises from evening off to nearest million and from short cuts in technique.

to calendar 1941 incomes), about $2.6 billion for fiscal 1943, and possibly $2.9 billion for fiscal 1944.

Estate Tax and Gift Tax.—Another source is the estate tax and its accompanying gift tax. Table 8 shows the total of net taxable estates, after deduction of the $40,000 exemption ($50,000 in a few cases), rearranged into brackets as the surtax net income was rearranged in Table 5.[11] The data represent all taxable returns filed during the calendar year 1938. They probably represent a fairly even mixture of calendar 1936 and 1937 economic conditions with some influence of even earlier years.

This table shows, for instance, that all the estates of more than $1 million had altogether $98 million falling in the range, or bracket, $1 million to $1.5 million. Some of this $98 million was contributed by estates of more than $1 million but less than $1.5 million, some by the still larger estates.

About one third ($628 million) of the total net estate falls in the range below $100,000. Somewhat more than another third ($701 million) falls in the net estate range of $100,000 to $1 million. Altogether, there was $1.7 billion of taxable net estate.

Table 9 shows a hypothetical scale of estate tax rates that, while certainly severe, may be useful for illustrative purposes, to show what would be required if half a billion dollars or so were to be obtained from this source simpy by raising rates. Table 9 also shows the present scale of rates.

This rate scale, like that of the income tax, may look more severe than it really is, since it shows bracket rates, not over-all average rates. Under this hypothetical scale an estate of $100,000 (net, but before the exemption), for instance, would pay 12.8 percent in tax:

[11] Derived from Table 2, *Statistics of Income,* 1937, p. 54.

TABLE 9

HYPOTHETICAL AND PRESENT FEDERAL ESTATE TAX RATES

Range, or Bracket, of Estate after All Deductions Including the Exemption of $40,000 (Dollars)	*Hypothetical Scale of Rates (Each Rate is Applicable Only to Corresponding Bracket of Estate, Not to Taxpayer's Entire Estate) (Percent)*	*Present Rate Scale (Including 10 Percent Increase Due to Defense Tax) (Each Rate Is Applicable Only to Corresponding Bracket of Estate) (Percent)*
0– 10,000	15	2.2
10,000– 20,000	17	4.4
20,000– 30,000	19	6.6
30,000– 40,000	22	8.8
40,000– 50,000	25	11.0
50,000– 70,000	30	13.2
70,000– 100,000	37	15.4
100,000– 200,000	45	18.7
200,000– 400,000	55	22.0
400,000– 600,000	65	25.3
600,000– 800,000	70	28.6
800,000– 1,000,000	75	31.9
1,000,000– 1,500,000	80	35.2
1,500,000– 2,000,000	80	38.5
2,000,000– 2,500,000	80	41.8
2,500,000– 3,000,000	80	45.1
3,000,000– 3,500,000	80	48.4
3,500,000– 4,000,000	80	51.7
4,000,000– 4,500,000	80	55.0
4,500,000– 5,000,000	80	58.3
5,000,000– 6,000,000	80	61.6
6,000,000– 7,000,000	80	64.9
7,000,000– 8,000,000	80	67.1
8,000,000– 9,000,000	80	69.3
9,000,000–10,000,000	80	71.5
10,000,000–20,000,000	80	73.7
20,000,000–50,000,000	80	75.9
Over 50,000,000	80	77.0

Estate, after all deductions but before the flat exemption	$100,000
Subtract $40,000 exemption	40,000
	$60,000
Tax on the $60,000, under hypothetical rate scale	$12,800

An estate of $1 million (net, but before the exemption) would pay 57.2 percent in tax, under this hypothetical scale.

If the hypothetical rate scale in Table 9 is applied to the bracket distribution of estates shown in Table 8, it will be found that the increase in revenue over the present rates is $450 million. Perhaps not more than $200 million of this could be reflected in the revenues of fiscal 1942 even if the rate-change were made effective at once (June, 1941), in view of the delay allowed in the payment of the tax.[12] A corresponding increase in the gift tax would not yield enough to affect appreciably the round figures used in the present analysis.

As with the income tax, certain adjustments to close loopholes would increase the yield substantially, but only after several years had elapsed.[13] No ready basis exists for estimating the fiscal effect of these measures, but tentatively they may be set at $100 million by the end of the decade (and assuming that the hypothetical rate scale or its equivalent will be in force).

By cutting the exemption from $40,000 to $20,000, another $100 million, more or less, might be obtained from old and new taxpayers—possibly nearer $200 million if the de-

[12] Even the $200 million estimate is too high unless the period allowed for payment is shortened, or at least unless there is removed the inducement to wait twelve months that is now provided by the optional valuation clause (at the taxpayer's option the value of the estate a year after death may be taken).

[13] For a statement and analysis of these adjustments, see C. Lowell Harriss, *Gift Taxation in the United States*, Washington, 1940.

crease were made under the rate increase and adjustments discussed above.[14]

In general, the series of measures just noted might increase the revenue from the estate tax and the gift tax by $200 million in fiscal 1942, $500 million in fiscal 1943, and $850 million in fiscal 1944. These estimates are even more uncertain than those under the income tax. They are more likely overstatements than understatements, especially since they reflect security prices of 1937, which were above those currently prevailing.

The Net Result of the First Set of Tax Changes.—The figures of total tax revenue, and of deficit, for 1941–44 may be revised as in Table 10 to reflect the changes in the individual income tax, the corporation income tax, and the estate and gift taxes described thus far—the first set of changes.

The data in Table 10 indicate that the considerable effort involved in the first set of tax changes would increase the revenues not at all in fiscal 1941, $1.6 billion in fiscal 1942, $3.1 billion in fiscal 1943, and $3.7 billion in fiscal 1944. These amounts, incidentally, are somewhat smaller than the $2.2 billion for fiscal 1942 and $3.6 billion for fiscal 1943 that are expected under the Treasury proposal (including increases in excise taxes) submitted recently.[15]

The annual deficit would rise to a peak of $14.2 billion in fiscal 1943 and drop to $2.7 billion in 1944, after the saving in interest noted below is taken into account.

Projection of these figures into fiscal years beyond fiscal

[14] The recent Treasury proposal to increase the estate tax rates (by amounts much less than those given in Table 9) and the gift tax rates and to lower the exemption to $25,000 and to lower the insurance exclusion also to $25,000 has been estimated to yield $347 million in a full fiscal year. Sullivan, *loc. cit.* No closing of other loopholes is reflected in this estimate. The yield estimated in the text above therefore cannot be checked satisfactorily by referring to the Treasury's figure.

[15] Sullivan, *loc. cit.*

Table 10

EXPENDITURES, TAX REVENUES, AND DEFICITS, FISCAL 1941–44, UNDER THE FIRST SET OF CHANGES IN INCOME AND ESTATE AND GIFT TAXES

(In Billions of Dollars)

	1941	*1942*	*1943*	*1944*
Expenditures (Table 2)	12.6	23.1	28.6	19.2
Revenues, before hypothetical changes (Table 4)	8.3	10.1	11.3	12.7
Revenues added by hypothetical changes:				
Individual income tax		*1.1*	*2.1*	*2.3*
Corporation income tax		*0.3*	*0.5*	*0.6*
Estate tax and gift tax		*0.2*	*0.5*	*0.8*
Total		1.6	3.1	3.7
Revenues, after hypothetical changes	8.3	11.7	14.4	16.4
Deficit, annual	4.3	11.4	14.2	2.8 [a]
Deficit, cumulative		15.7	29.9	32.7
Total Federal debt, direct and guaranteed, excluding part of the debt held in Federal government accounts at the end of the fiscal year [b]	51.0	62.4	76.6	79.4 [a]

[a] The 1944 figure is to be decreased by $0.1 billion if the saving in interest in 1944 is taken into account. The cumulative saving in interest would be $0.2 billion.

[b] Starting from a figure of $46.7 billion as of June 30, 1940. For the derivation of this figure, see Appendix 2.

1944 may be useful if it is recognized as being by no means a prediction but simply an illustration of one of many possibilities. In terms of the general perspective that is being attempted here, the revenues for 1945–52 may be modified to read, in round numbers (billions), $15, $13, $11, $11, $13, $14, and $15 respectively,[16] an increase of $3, $3, $2, $2, $2, $3, and $3 billion respectively. The added tax revenues would decrease somewhat the load on the budget for interest. At 2 percent interest the saving would accumulate to approximately $2.5 billion over the period 1942–51, starting at less than one tenth of a billion a year and gradually increasing to about half a billion a year in 1951. Hence the total decrease in the deficits for 1945–51, from what they would be if the tax system were not strengthened at all, would be, to the nearest billion, the same as the figures of revenue increase given immediately above, except that another billion might be added for 1948 and 1951. The deficits for 1945–51 would therefore be, to the nearest billion, zero, $3, $6, $6, $2, $2, and zero. Therefore, despite the effort reflected by the first set of tax changes, (a) there would be a Federal deficit in all but two (1945, 1951) of the fiscal years 1941 to 1951 inclusive; (b) the cumulative deficit for the eleven-year period would be $50 billion—$32 billion, 1941–44 inclusive, plus $18 billion in 1945–51 inclusive; (c) if the cumulative deficit were met wholly by borrowing, the Federal debt (other than debt held by Federal government itself), direct and guaranteed, would have increased from $46.7 billion on June 30, 1940, to $97 billion on June 30, 1951; [17] (d) as of the end of 1951 there would be little pros-

[16] If these seem somewhat low, especially in view of the growth in population, other factors must be recalled; for instance, the high rates of income tax will diminish the estates available for taxation in later years.

[17] Although the guaranteed debt is ignored in computing interest charges, it is best included in statements of the debt outstanding, since the data presented later on banks, insurance companies, etc., are more significant if the

pect that the growth in the debt would be stopped even temporarily, since 1950 and 1951 represent, under the assumptions used, peak years of prosperity.

FURTHER INCREASES IN THE PERSONAL INCOME TAX

The conclusions of the preceding section do not, of course, indicate that the Federal budget cannot be balanced by an increase in taxes. They probably do indicate that a balance would not be achieved, except in peak years of peacetime prosperity, without a program of somewhat more severe tax increases than those postulated in the first set above. This first set, it will be recalled, is slightly less severe than the tax bill that is now being drafted by the Ways and Means Committee of the House; the former would raise $3.1 billion additional revenue in fiscal 1943; the latter, about $3.5 billion. A stabilization of the Federal debt (that is, years of surplus to offset years of deficit) would not occur without a much more severe increase in taxation than that provided by the current tax bill. And the stabilization could not occur below a level of debt much higher than the present one. A substantial permanent reduction of the debt, even at any time beyond 1945, would involve tax measures whose magnitude can be only dimly perceived. Moreover, it must be kept in mind that the conclusions can be only tentative, since they are based on the price levels assumed in Table 3. The pro-

---

entire Federal debt, direct and guaranteed, is studied. For the derivation of the $46.7-billion figure see Appendix 2. It includes $5.5 billion guaranteed debt. Figures for future years assume that this $5.5 billion figure will remain unchanged. This probably leads to some overstatement of the total debt. The debt of the Home Owners Loan Corporation, which accounts for $2.6 billion of the guaranteed debt, is being reduced. On the other hand, it was stated recently that Federal corporations and credit agencies would be in the market, during fiscal 1942, for about $1.0 billion of short-term money (Under Secretary Bell, as reported in the New York *Sun*, May 7, 1941, p. 42). All in all, the best procedure for the purposes of the present study seems to be to assume that the $5.5 billion figure will remain unchanged.

spective minimum deficit for fiscal 1943 is about $14 billion even with the present tax system strengthened by $3.5 billion for that year. The nonfiscal controls that could keep the price level down to the figures of Table 3 in the face of this deficit would have to be severe indeed. A substantial rise in the price level would itself affect government revenues and government expenditures and hence the size of the deficit.

Lowering the Exemptions under the Personal Income Tax.—The exemption for a single person was lowered from $1,000 to $800 under the Revenue Act of 1940. Actually, because of the 10 percent deduction allowed under the earned income credit, and because the law declares that income from whatever source shall be deemed earned income up to $3,000, the single person pays no tax unless his net income exceeds $889. The exemption for a married couple or a head of a family was decreased from $2,500 to $2,000; the lowest taxable level actually is $2,223, because of the earned income credit. Congress may not want to lower the exemptions still further until at least a few months' experience has been gained in the administration at the new levels. This point alone would not deter the submission of estimates here; two other factors are decisive in the present case for omitting them. First, the computation of the revenue that would be obtained from new taxpayers—those with incomes too low to be reached under the tax as it now stands—is a laborious process, full of pitfalls. Second, the amount of such revenue would probably be insignificant for purposes of the data given here, in tenths of billions, unless the initial tax rate were set at a very high level—say 15 or 20 percent—and even then the over-all results would not be changed significantly unless the exemptions were reduced drastically.[18] With respect to

[18] See, for instance, the last column in Table III of "Revenue Possibilities of the Personal Income Tax," by Walter A. Durham, Jr., and Grover William Ensley, in *Bulletin of the National Tax Association,* May, 1940, p. 234.

the increased revenue that would come from those who already pay a tax (a lowering of the exemptions of course increases the tax due from all taxpayers), a hypothetical increase in the surtax rates with the existing exemptions will do just as well for the purpose of computing revenue possibilities.

If the exemptions were lowered drastically—say, to $500 for single persons and $1,200 for married couples—and if the initial rate were 15 or 20 percent, the revenue results would indeed be important. It is to be hoped that estimates for such a measure will be forthcoming in some future study. With any such estimate, the question of collection at the source would have to be considered. Meanwhile, this possibility cannot be developed here in quantitative terms.

An income tax with no exemptions whatever, collected at the source as much as possible, poses administrative difficulties so severe that there is little point in trying to make revenue estimates for it until careful study has indicated the size of the areas over which an almost complete breakdown of administration might result. Moreover, the desired revenue and desired decrease in civilian consumption can doubtless be obtained without imposing so severe a burden on those of very low incomes, that is, those below, say, $750 a year (these low-income consumers accounted for only about 13 percent of the total consumption in the United States in 1935-36).[19]

Increases in Surtax Rates Up to $20,000.—The income ranges immediately above the present exemption levels would still contain a considerable amount of net income after tax,

[19] National Resources Committee, *Consumer Expenditures in the United States,* Table 32-A. For these reasons, the estimates given by Professor Lutz, in his proposal of this kind of tax, are not utilized in these computations. See H. L. Lutz, *Financing the Defense Program,* pub. by National Economy League, 1941; "Financing the Defense Program," *Bulletin of the National Tax Association,* Feb., 1941.

in terms of aggregate absolute amount, even after applying the hypothetical rate scale in the first set of tax changes. Thus the bracket of zero to $2,000 surtax net income (corresponding for instance to a $2,000 to $4,000 net-income range for a married couple without dependents, and to an $800 to $2,800 net-income range for a single person without dependents) contained $4.4 billion of surtax net income in 1937; the hypothetical surtax scale in Table 6 would take $0.4 billion of that. The existing normal tax of 4.4 percent (assumed unchanged in this discussion) would take perhaps another $0.2 billion (the precise amount is not evident, owing to the earned-income and government-bond exemptions), leaving $3.8 billion. Similarly, in the bracket of $2,000 to $4,000 surtax net income, about $1.0 billion would be left. And as the examples of pages 35–36 and Table 7 show, the tax due under the hypothetical scale on the incomes below $5,000 is far from crushing. These considerations make it worth while to explore the revenue possibilities of a "second set" of tax changes that will consist simply of a further increase in personal income tax surtax rates on the levels below, say, $20,000. A second hypothetical rate scale constructed on this basis is presented in Table 11, which also shows the first hypothetical scale and the present scale—surtax rates only.

In the second hypothetical surtax rate scale, the initial bracket rate is 20 percent, and the bracket rates are higher than those of the first hypothetical rate scale up to the $20,000 surtax net income level (the amount of tax due, of course, increases for all taxpayers). Under this scale, the normal tax plus surtax on the married taxpayer with two dependents and a net income of $3,000 would be $40 (instead of $20 as under the first hypothetical scale)—1⅓ percent of his net income. The same taxpayer with $5,000 net income would pay $524.80 in Federal income tax—about

10½ percent of his net income, instead of 6 percent as under the first scale. At $20,000 of net income he would pay $6,523.20 tax (instead of $4,755.20 under the first hypo-

TABLE 11

FIRST AND SECOND HYPOTHETICAL AND PRESENT SURTAX RATE SCALES [a]

Range, or Bracket, of Surtax Net Income (Net Income after Deducting Personal Exemption and Credit for Dependents) (Dollars)	*Second Hypothetical Scale (Percent)*	*First Hypothetical Scale (from Table 6) (Percent)*	*Present Scale (Including 10 Percent Increase Due to Defense Tax) (Percent)*
0– 2,000	20	10	0.0
2,000– 4,000	25	13	0.0
4,000– 6,000	30	16	4.4
6,000– 8,000	34	20	6.6
8,000–10,000	36	24	8.8
10,000–12,000	38	28	11.0
12,000–14,000	40	32	13.2
14,000–16,000	42	36	16.5
16,000–18,000	44	40	19.8
18,000–20,000	46	44	23.1
Above 20,000	Same as first hypothetical scale	(see Table 6)	(see Table 6)

[a] Each rate is applicable only to corresponding bracket of income, not to taxpayer's entire income.

thetical set of rates), or roughly 33 percent of his income. All of these percentages would be appreciably higher for taxpayers with fewer dependents, especially single taxpayers.

The individual income tax under this second hypothetical surtax scale plus the existing normal tax is appreciably heavier than the current Treasury proposal. For a married couple with no dependents, for instance, it takes $111 from a $2,500 income, compared with $72 tax under the Treasury proposal. At $3,000 it takes $231 (Treasury proposal, $152). At $4,000 it takes $470; at $5,000 it takes $760; at $6,000 it takes $1,050. At the $8,000 level the tax increases to $1,729; and at the $10,000 level, to $2,488—about 25 percent of the income. At $12,500 the tax is $3,497; at $15,000, it is $4,570; and at $20,000, it is $6,910—over one third of the income. Reference to Table 7 will show that these amounts are all substantially above the proposals that are being currently discussed.

Net Result of the Second Set of Tax Changes.—Applied to the 1937 surtax income as shown in Table 5, this second hypothetical surtax rate scale gives an increase in yield of $893 million over the first hypothetical scale—perhaps $1.1 billion for the year of intense business activity that would be reflected in fiscal 1942, and $1.2 billion for fiscal 1943, assuming that the other adjustments under the first set of tax changes had been made. An allowance for the decrease in dividend income caused by the postulated increase in the corporation tax would not be significant in terms of tenths of billions. About $0.6 billion might be received in fiscal 1942 if the change were made applicable to calendar 1941 incomes. Then the "revenues" figures in Table 10 would become, for 1941–44 (in billions), $8.3, $12.3, $15.6, and $17.7 respectively.[20] A further saving in interest would result, ranging from $5 million in fiscal 1942 (½ of 2 percent of $600 million) to $200 million in fiscal 1951, and aggregating about $1.0 billion over the eleven-year period. For simplicity in estimating, this entire billion may be allocated to 1951. The deficits for the eleven-year period then become (in billions) $4.3, $11, $13, $1, $–1, $2, $5, $5, $1, $1, and $–2. Hence, the budget would show a surplus in 1945 and 1951. The cumulative deficit for the eleven-year period

[20] See Table 12 (p. 62) for estimated additional revenues from this source in future years.

would be $39 billion—$29 billion in 1941–44 and $10 billion in 1945–51. If this deficit were met wholly by borrowing, the Federal debt (other than debt held by the Federal government), direct and guaranteed, would have increased from $46.7 billion on June 30, 1940, to about $86 billion.

General Summary of the Result under the First and Second Tax Changes.—The computations up to this point probably justify a general conclusion something like this: If Federal expenditures over the next decade are about as set forth in Table 2, and if there were enacted at once a revenue-raising measure involving an initial bracket rate of 24.4 percent under the personal income tax, with bracket rates rising to about 40 percent in the $8,000 to $10,000 range, about 50 percent in the $18,000 to $20,000 range, and about 65 percent in the $44,000 to $50,000 range, and involving, too, an increase of 6 percentage points in the corporate income tax rate scale and a steep increase in the estate tax (starting with a 15 percent bracket rate and reaching a 30 percent bracket rate in the $50,000 to $70,000 range, and an 80 percent rate in the $1 million to $1.5 million range, for instance), and including an elimination of major loopholes under both taxes and an increase in the gift tax, the budget would show moderate surpluses in two out of the eleven years 1941–51, moderate deficits in four others, and substantial deficits in the other five, the direct and guaranteed debt held by the public increasing from $46.7 billion (June 30, 1940) to about $86 billion (June 30, 1951).

SALES TAXES

Another source to which Congress may turn for revenue is the family of sales taxes—manufacturers' excises, manufacturers' sales tax, retail sales tax, general turnover tax, and so on.

Excises on Particular Products.—Only a few excises on

particular products can yield enough to be significant for purposes of the present analysis. Most of the single-commodity excises applied in this country or other countries are unimportant with respect to yield, even at rates as high as feasible from an administrative viewpoint. The current Treasury proposal to raise $3.6 billion in added revenue includes thirty excise items (new excises or increases in old ones), but four out of the thirty produce half of the total increase (gasoline, $255 million; distilled spirits, $135 million; soft drinks, $132 million; cigarettes, $125 million). Virtually all of the rest is accounted for by eight items: tobacco products other than cigarettes, beer, automobiles (including parts and accessories), checks, admissions, tires and tubes, telephone, etc., and passenger transportation.

The present study is dealing only in tenths of billions of dollars—primarily, indeed, in billions. It may therefore dispense with all but the few large-yielding excises—those on cigarettes, distilled spirits, beer, gasoline, automobiles, and soft drinks. The tax rates and estimates of yield to be given here do not imply that these taxes are particularly suitable; in fact, they have two disadvantages not possessed by a general type of tax such as the income tax or the general sales tax. They weigh very heavily, perhaps unfairly so, on a few producers because of the fall in consumption that results from the rise in price caused by the tax; thus stockholders, managers, and employees in the cigarette, distilled spirits, and similarly taxed industries are called on to make a special sacrifice not asked of stockholders, employees, and so on in other industries. Second, it is not evident that the particular plant, materials, workers, and management that are made idle by this fall in consumption will be of special use in the production of defense articles—excepting, of course, automobiles and possibly petroleum. Manufacturers' excise taxes need to be approached from a new point of view, in the light of the defense program, to ascertain how they may be used to check civilian consumption of a kind that interferes with defense and how they may recapture for the government the windfall profits that may accrue to the producers of, and dealers in, the scarce articles. These aspects, however, are not treated at length here, since they are usually not significant in terms of billions or even tenths of billions of revenue.

The tobacco tax is estimated to yield slightly more than $700 million in fiscal 1942, of which over $600 million comes from the tax of 6½ cents per package of cigarettes. Under drastic pressure the cigarette tax could yield a few hundred million more, but it must be recalled that twenty-nine states and some cities now tax cigarettes and received nearly $100 million from that source in 1940. The tax goes as high as 5 cents in three states, Arkansas, Louisiana, and Oklahoma, making the aggregate tax there 11½ cents; the total may reach still higher levels in some states where local units also tax cigarettes.[21] If the Federal tax were increased about 3 cents, the added yield might be about $200 million a year. The increase of 1½ cents recently recommended by the Treasury is estimated to yield $125 million. The taxes on cigars, smoking tobacco, and so on, could be increased, but the revenue would probably not be significant for purposes of the present rough computations. A doubling of the tax rates would produce $76 million, the Treasury has estimated.

The liquor taxes now in force are estimated to yield $840 million in fiscal 1942, somewhat more than half of this coming from the distilled spirits tax of $3 a proof-gallon and somewhat less than half from the beer tax of $6 a barrel.

Distilled spirits might yield a few hundred million more, but state taxation is virtually universal and fairly heavy. In New York, where the state tax is relatively high ($1.50 per gallon), the combined Federal and state tax represents

[21] Public Administration Clearing House, *News Bulletin*, June 10, 1941.

about half the price to the consumer on the less expensive brands.[22] An increase in the Federal tax of about $1.50 a gallon might produce about $200 million in revenue. The Federal beer tax, when added to a fairly typical state tax on beer, represents about a sixth to a quarter of the price to the consumer.[23] If a tax increase of about 75 percent were imposed, the yield might rise nearly $200 million.

The present Federal gasoline tax of 1½ cents a gallon is yielding $400 million a year. Another $400 million might be obtained by increasing the tax by 2 cents; whether Congress would want to go this far, or beyond, may be doubtful in view of the state taxes, commonly around 4 or 5 cents a gallon.

The present taxes of 3½ percent on passenger automobiles and motorcycles and 2½ percent on parts and accessories were estimated (in the last budget document) to yield $85 million in fiscal 1942, and the Treasury has recently suggested that $78 million more be raised by doubling these rates. The requirements of the defense program seem to indicate a need for a much greater curtailment of production of automobiles than would be brought about by so small a tax increase. If such a curtailment does develop, prices of automobiles will rise—if not manufacturers' prices, the prices charged by dealers, or, if dealers are restrained, then prices among individuals buying and selling cars to each other. Large windfall profits would thereby result. The government could to a large extent take this profit by levying on the manufacturers an excise high enough to force the manufacturers' prices to a level that would leave less room for big profit spreads farther down the line. Just how high that excise rate would have to be cannot be computed here, but

[22] C. Lowell Harriss, "Enigma of Tax Rate Differentials," *Liquor Taxes and Public Welfare* (pub. by the *Journal of Commerce*, Jan. 24, 1941) p. 25.

[23] *Ibid.*

for illustrative purposes it may be assumed that a 20 percent tax is imposed and produces $0.3 billion altogether, or an increase of $0.2 billion over the present tax.

The soft drinks tax recently proposed by the Treasury—one cent a bottle, and equivalents on unbottled drinks—is estimated to yield $132 million a year but will not be considered here for two reasons: the tax might not be able to yield a great deal more than that amount, no matter how high the rate was put, and the problem of imposing an equivalent tax on unbottled drinks (or the materials used in making them) is a difficult one.

A summation of the tax increases above gives an average annual increase of $1.2 billion for the "third set" of tax changes. But the fact that the tax was increased on one article would in itself tend to decrease the consumer's ability to pay the increased taxes on the other commodities, so that a simple adding of the figures is not a safe procedure. This aspect is intensified if it is proposed to add all these increases to the increases in income tax and estate tax discussed above. In general, under the rate increases just described, it is not safe to count on more than a billion dollars extra, annually, over the eleven-year period, even when allowing for the growth in population. This added billion (disregarding fluctuations above and below that average) would increase the revenue figures as given on page 51, for 1941–44, to (in billions) $8.3, $13.3, $16.6, and $18.7 and for 1945–51 they might be (in billions) $18, $15, $13, $13, $15, $16, and $17. Again, this would save about a billion in interest charges over the period, which may be arbitrarily allocated to fiscal 1950 for convenience in computation, and the deficits would drop to $4.3, $9.8, and (to nearest billion) $12, zero, $-2, $1, $4, $4, zero, $-2, and $-3. The cumulative deficit thus becomes $28 billion, and the Federal direct and guaranteed debt privately held would have increased from $46.7 billion (1940) to $75 billion (1951).

The total figure for these special excises over the entire eleven-year period is of restricted significance in that some of these measures, particularly the tax on automobiles, would surely not be continued in the event of a depression. But this is a minor phase of the larger problem of how the structure of the tax system might be altered when depression strikes, and the statements on pages 27 above and 67 below may be referred to at this point.

Manufacturers' Sales Tax.—Of the more general types of sales tax, the kind that is restricted to manufacturers' sales is the most commonly discussed in this country so far as the Federal government is concerned. It might be imposed on the full value of each sale by every manufacturer, including sales of partly finished products by one manufacturer to another, but this would give the vertically integrated firm a big tax advantage. Hence the tax would probably take either one of the two following forms: a tax on the full value of all sales of finished articles by manufacturers to wholesalers, retailers, or consumers (the "last" manufacturers would thus be the only ones taxed); or a tax on the value added by each manufacturer as the article progressed onward from the early raw-material stage to the finished-product stage. The value-added tax would yield less than the tax on finished products at the same rate unless the former also applied to the value of the raw materials at the first stage. The yield of a tax on finished products cannot be estimated directly from the totals given in the *Census of Manufactures.* The "value of products" total ($61 billion in 1937) may be used only for a tax that would apply to every sale by every manufacturer, not merely by the manufacturers of finished products. The "value added" figure is too low, since it excludes the value of the raw materials. There is some evidence that the value of the finished products is about two thirds of the total "value of products."[24] If this is so, the finished products might total about $40 billion for 1937. Translating this to 1941 and following years is hazardous; wholesale prices are now at the level of 1937, and activity is greater. Much of the activity, however, is in producing armaments, uniforms, food, and so forth, for sale to the Federal government under the huge defense program, and presumably the government would not put a tax on its own purchases. Some allowance must be made for difficulties in administering a new tax, for repercussions of the tax on business activity, and for the effects exercised by the assumed prior tax increases. For the present rough computations, these factors may be considered to offset each other, leaving the tax base $40 billion for fiscal 1942 and about $44 billion for fiscal 1943 and 1944, under the price levels assumed. Therefore a 4 percent tax might yield as much as $1.7 billion in a high-price-level high-production year (1943, in these computations).

If food were exempted, the tax base would be decreased by about one fourth,[25] to $30 billion for fiscal 1942 and $33 billion for 1943 and 1944. A 4 percent rate would yield $1.2 billion on the $30-billion base. To allow for some delay in getting administration of the tax fully under way, and since the tax could scarcely be drafted and enacted with the requisite care in time to get the full twelve months' collections in fiscal 1942, a figure of $0.9 billion is given for that year. Figures for later years are shown in Table 12. The exemption of food is assumed both because there would probably be more general interest in this kind of tax and because that

[24] Bureau of the Census, U.S. Department of Commerce, *Census of Manufactures, 1937,* p. 9.

[25] Based on computations in an unpublished manuscript available at the writer's office.

exemption would appreciably lessen the pressure on those of very low incomes. It has been estimated that families and single individuals with incomes between $750 and $1,000 devote 40 percent of their entire expenditure to food and 19 percent to rent.[26] The percentages are somewhat higher for those with still lower incomes.

On the basis of these figures, the revenue data on page 56 for 1941–44 would then be (in billions) $8.3, $14.2, $17.9, and $20.0 and for 1945–51 they might be $19, $16, $14, $14, $16, $17, and $18. Allowing for another billion dollars' saving in interest, which may be arbitrarily allocated to fiscal 1949, the deficits would drop to $4.3, $8.9, and (to nearest billion) $11, $–1, $–3, zero, $3, $3, $–2, $–3, and $–5. The cumulative deficit is thus $17 billion for the eleven-year period, and the Federal direct and guaranteed debt privately held would have increased from $46.7 billion (1940) to $64 billion (1951). The debt would have reached a peak of $70 billion by June 30, 1943.

At this point, however, it is again necessary to recall that these figures would be altered by any changes in the price level and degree of business activity that were assumed in Table 3. In the earlier stages of this analysis it was pointed out that if the tax system were strengthened not at all or only moderately, the price level would rise substantially, in the absence of strict controls. Now the opposite danger is approached—the possibility that, as tax increase is piled on tax increase, business activity in the later years of the decade would not be enough to produce the national income totals of Table 3.

Whether the tax load would keep the price level below the figures of Table 3 is more doubtful; indeed, some taxes will probably tend to increase the price level above what it would

[26] National Resources Committee, *Consumer Expenditures in the United States*, p. 85.

be if the money were obtained by borrowing (even by borrowing at the commercial banks), or at least will keep the price level just as high, over the short term. Any taxes that operate to increase business costs immediately may have this effect —a general sales tax, for example. Business concerns in general have easy access to the credit market and might put up prices by a degree roughly equal to the tax, even at the cost (a cost perhaps not closely reckoned) of cutting down the physical volume of business. On the other hand, government borrowing may indeed carry a secondary, subsequent, stimulus to a price rise that a business tax would not. More important, perhaps, is the fact that, even with all four tax changes in force, the deficits for fiscal 1942 and fiscal 1943 would be large—$9 billion and $11 billion respectively. In any case, careful computation of the net result, and hence of the degree to which the Table 3 assumptions can be held valid under severe tax increases, must be put aside in the present study as unfinished business.

PAYROLL TAXES

The present law provides that the payroll tax for old-age benefits, now one percent on employers plus one percent on employees, shall rise to 2 percent on each for the calendar years 1943–45, 2½ percent for 1946–48, and 3 percent for 1949 and the years following. Up to this point in the present discussion it has been assumed that the rate would stay at one percent on each. Experience gives some basis for this assumption; under the Act of August 14, 1935, the rate for the calendar years 1940, 1941, and 1942 was scheduled to rise to 1½ percent, but the Act of August 10, 1939, eliminated this increase. The recent budget estimate for these two one-percent taxes for fiscal 1942 was $725 million (it was $668 million for fiscal 1941), and if the figures in Table 12 are assumed, the scheduled increases give, in billions, an additional $0.3 for fiscal 1943, $0.8 for 1944, $0.8 for 1945, $1.0 for 1946, $1.1 for 1947 and again $1.1 for 1948 (1947 and 1948 being assumed somewhat depressed), $1.4 for 1949, and $1.6 for 1950 and 1951. Under these assumptions the revenue figures on page 59 for 1941–44 would be (in billions) $8.3, $14.2, $18.2, and $20.8, and for 1945–51 they might be (to nearest billion) $19, $17, $15, $15, $17, $19, and $20—an aggregate increase of some $10 billion. Allowing for still another billion dollars of savings in interest, which this time may be arbitrarily allocated to 1948, the deficits would drop to $4.3, $8.9, and (to nearest billion) $10, $-2, $-4, $-1, $2, $1, $-3, $-4, and $-6. The aggregate effect of these tax changes would thus be a deficit of $6 billion for the period 1941–51, and the Federal direct and guaranteed debt—privately held—would be changed from the $47 billion level of 1940 to $53 billion in 1951. It would rise to a peak of $70 billion at the end of fiscal 1943 and be reduced by surpluses in all succeeding years except 1947 and 1948.

The warning at the end of the discussion of the sales tax above must, of course, be repeated here with added force, with respect to the later years of the decade; for fiscal 1942 and 1943 the deficits are still large—$9 billion and $10 billion respectively.

GENERAL SUMMARY OF ALL TAX INCREASES

The cumulative results reached in these computations for the gigantic tax program implied by the five sets of tax changes discussed above are shown in Table 12. For the convenience of the reader who wishes to trace the changes in the assumed deficits, the data of Table 13 are given. Too much importance can easily be attached to totals like these, in view of the possibility that the heavy load of these tax measures would make untenable the national income assumptions of Table 3 with respect to the later years of the decade.

TABLE 12

FEDERAL REVENUES UNDER THE ASSUMPTION OF ALL FIVE SETS OF TAX CHANGES, 1941–51

(In Billions of Dollars)

	1941	*1942*	*1943*	*1944*	*1945*	*1946*	*1947*	*1948*	*1949*	*1950*	*1951*	*Total 1941–51*
Revenues under present system (Table 4)	8.3	10.1	11.3	12.7	12.2	10.4	9.0	9.1	10.3	11.2	11.7	116.3
First set of tax changes:												
Individual income tax: surtax rates (Table 6) and loopholes		1.1	2.1	2.3								
Corporation income tax, 6 points increase		0.3	0.5	0.6								
Estate tax and gift tax: rates (Table 9) and loopholes		0.2	0.5	0.8								
Total, first set [a]		*1.6*	*3.1*	*3.7*	*3.3*	*2.5*	*2.1*	*1.9*	*2.4*	*2.9*	*3.1*	*26.6*
Second set: further increase in surtax rates (Table 11)		*0.6*	*1.2*	*1.3*	*1.2*	*0.9*	*0.8*	*0.8*	*0.9*	*1.0*	*1.1*	*9.8*
Third set: [b] Spirits, increase $1.50 a gallon		0.2	0.2	0.2	0.2	0.2	0.2	0.2	0.2	0.2	0.2	
Beer, increase $4.50 a barrel		0.2	0.2	0.2	0.2	0.2	0.2	0.2	0.2	0.2	0.2	
Cigarettes, increase 3 cents a package		0.2	0.2	0.2	0.2	0.2	0.2	0.2	0.2	0.2	0.2	

Gasoline, increase 2 cents a gallon		0.4	0.4	0.4	0.4	0.4	0.4	0.4	0.4	0.4	0.4	
Automobiles, increase 16½ percentage points		0.2	0.2	0.2	0.2	0.2	0.2	0.2	0.2	0.2	0.2	
Total, third set, after allowances		*1.0*	*1.0*	*1.0*	*1.0*	*1.0*	*1.0*	*1.0*	*1.0*	*1.0*	*1.0*	*10.0*
Fourth set: Manufacturers' sales tax, 4% on value of finished articles, food exempt		*0.9*	*1.3*	*1.3*	*1.0*	*0.9*	*0.8*	*0.9*	*1.0*	*1.1*	*1.1*	*10.3*
Fifth set: payroll taxes increase according to schedule			*0.3*	*0.8*	*0.8*	*1.0*	*1.1*	*1.1*	*1.4*	*1.6*	*1.6*	*9.7*
Total increase from five sets		4.1	6.9	8.1	7.3	6.3	5.8	5.7	6.7	7.6	7.9	66.4
Total revenue including revenue from five sets	8.3	14.2	18.2	20.8	19.5	16.7	14.8	14.8	17.0	18.8	19.6	182.7
Total revenue, to nearest billion	8	14	18	21	20	17	15	15	17	19	20	183

[a] The revenue increases for 1945–51 were estimated for the three items as a whole and were assumed to vary proportionately with the changes in the yield of the income taxes of the existing system, as shown in Table 4, p. 23.

[b] As to why the total is somewhat less than the sum of the items, see text; also, the yields would actually fluctuate somewhat above and below the unchanging figures given here.

TABLE 13

ADDITIONS TO TAX REVENUE AND DECREASES IN DEFICITS (ALLOWING FOR SAVINGS IN INTEREST) ASSUMED UNDER THE FIVE SETS OF TAX CHANGES, 1941–51

	1941	*1942*	*1943*	*1944*	*1945*	*1946*	*1947*	*1948*	*1949*	*1950*	*1951*	*Total*
Deficit before changes	$4.3	13.0	17.3	6.5	3.8	5.6	8.0	8.0	4.7	4.8	3.3	$79.3
First set of tax changes	..	1.6	3.2 [a]	3.9 [a]	3.5 [a]	2.7 [a]	2.4 [a]	2.2 [a]	2.8 [a]	3.3 [a]	3.6 [a]	29.2
Deficit	4.3	11.4	14.1	2.6	0.3	2.9	5.6	5.8	1.9	1.5	−0.3	50.1
Second set of tax changes	..	0.6	1.2	1.3	1.2	0.9	0.8	0.8	0.9	1.0	2.1 [b]	10.8
Deficit	4.3	10.8	12.9	1.3	−0.9	2.0	4.8	5.0	1.0	0.5	−2.4	39.3
Third set of tax changes	..	1.0	1.0	1.0	1.0	1.0	1.0	1.0	1.0	2.0 [b]	1.0	11.0
Deficit	4.3	9.8	11.9	0.3	−1.9	1.0	3.8	4.0	0.0	−1.5	−3.4	28.3
Fourth set of tax changes	..	0.9	1.3	1.3	1.0	0.9	0.8	0.9	2.0 [b]	1.1	1.1	11.3
Deficit	4.3	8.9	10.6	−1.0	−2.9	0.1	3.0	3.1	−2.0	−2.6	−4.5	17.0
Fifth set of tax changes	..	..	0.3	0.8	0.8	1.0	1.1	2.1 [b]	1.4	1.6	1.6	10.7
Deficit	4.3	8.9	10.3	−1.8	−3.7	−0.9	1.9	1.0	−3.4	−4.2	−6.1	6.3

[a] Differs from the figures in Table 12 by the amount of the saving in interest.
[b] Includes interest saving of $1 billion allocated arbitrarily to this year.

On the other hand, the large deficits that remain for fiscal 1942 and fiscal 1943, even with all five sets of tax changes, indicate the possibility that (so far as these hypothetical tax measures alone are concerned) prices, the cost of living, and national income would not be kept from rising above the levels of Table 3. But the totals are presented nevertheless, since they may help to give a tentative sense of proportion.

Under these five sets of increases the additional Federal tax revenue would rise to a peak of $8 billion in fiscal 1944 and another peak of about $8 billion in 1951. The total Federal revenue would rise from $8 billion in fiscal 1941 to a peak of $21 billion in 1944, drop to $15 billion in 1947 and 1948, and rise to $20 billion in 1951. Meanwhile the states and localities would presumably raise at least $10 billion in taxes of their own,[27] so that in 1944 the total tax revenue would be at least $30 billion.

Several warnings to the reader are in order at this point:

1. The figures on revenues, expenditures, and deficits are not predictions of what will happen. They are simply estimates of what might reasonably be expected to happen *under a particular set of assumptions about national income, price levels, interest rates, and so on;* these assumptions are themselves dependent for their validity, as has been noted several times above, on what is done with respect to the tax system and the borrowing program. For instance, the national income might not reach the $90-billion level at the end of the decade under the load that would be imposed by all five sets of tax changes described above. Conversely, price inflation would probably boost it well above the $100-billion level in the next two or three years if no tax increases at all were made. Indeed, there seems to be a distinct possibility that even all five sets of tax increases would not in themselves pre-

[27] They raised about $9.2 billion in 1940. Bureau of the Census, U.S. Department of Commerce, *State Tax Collections: 1940,* p. 29.

vent a substantial increase in prices over the next two years, so large are the prospective deficits. Not only would changes in the national income affect the tax yield (to some extent, an attempt has been made to allow for this in setting down the figures); they would also affect the dollar volume of expenditures. Therefore, the figures up to this point need refinement in some subsequent study. Nevertheless, they serve a purpose in giving a tentative glimpse of the quantities involved.

2. The combined effect, on a given individual, of all these tax increases is difficult to comprehend quickly, and it would certainly vary greatly from taxpayer to taxpayer. Consider, for instance, a family, two dependents, $5,000 a year income from salary, consuming 300 packages of cigarettes a year, spending $2,000 on the kind of goods that would be subject to a manufacturers' sales tax if food were exempted,[28] buying $50 worth of spirits and beer, and using 500 gallons of gasoline. The personal income tax would increase from $74.80 to $524.80 (page 49 above)—an increase of $450. If the family did not reduce its consumption of cigarettes it would pay $9 a year more in tax on this item. Its liquor tax bill, already about $15 or $20, would be increased perhaps $10 or $15. The added gasoline tax would be $10 unless consumption were reduced (and some of the increased cost to business users of gasoline would trickle down to the consumer). Whether the automobile tax should be included would depend on the particular circumstances of the family. If the retail value of the articles subject to the manufacturers' sales tax averaged about twice as much as the value on which the 4 percent tax was based, the family would pay about $40 in

[28] See, e.g., Table 6-A in National Resources Committee's *Consumer Expenditures in the United States,* indicating that a family with $4,000 to $5,000 income spent 75 percent of its income on consumption goods, including 19 percent on food and 13 percent on housing, both of which would be exempt from the sales tax (though after several years the influence of the tax would begin to be felt in the supply of dwellings).

tax annually on this account. By 1949 the payroll tax increase would be at least 2 percent on $3,000 of salary, or $60, and possibly 4 percent, or $120, if the employers' tax also rested as a burden on this family. Thus the total tax increase for this family would be at least somewhere near $600, and possibly not far from $700, depending on the extent to which shifting of the excises operated (these calculations assume virtually complete shifting). For a family of this type, the income tax increase is the overshadowing item. In this computation the increases in the corporation tax and the estate tax are omitted as being not significant; they would have to be allowed for in the higher incomes. And in the lower incomes the increase in the other taxes would be more severe, in terms of percentage increase of total taxes already paid.

The present analysis of possible tax increases must stop at this point; but this is not to imply that still greater increases are either economically or politically impossible. Further possibilities need to be explored, especially for the fiscal years 1942, 1943, and 1944.

3. The analysis here assumes that the new tax measures will be continued unchanged throughout the defense boom and the hypothetical depression and revival following it. This assumption is a simplifying one, necessary in a study that is designed merely to give a general idea of the proportions involved. It should not be inferred that the tax system actually will remain throughout all those years with the additions made during the defense period. It may prove advisable to readjust the system to give private enterprise added incentive when peace returns; or, as some would argue, to readjust it to check private saving and encourage private spending. Whatever the reasons may prove to be, some change seems inevitable.[29]

[29] See pp. 27 and 57 above.

Chapter IV

BORROWING AT LOW RATES OF INTEREST

THE CUMULATIVE deficits for the eleven-year period, under the basic assumptions on pages 13–16, range from $50 billion under the first set of tax increases to $6 billion, under the five sets. For the shorter period, the fiscal years 1941–1943, inclusive, the deficits range from $30 billion under the first set of additional taxes to $23 billion under the five sets. The first set, it will be recalled, is only slightly less productive than the revenue bill that Congress is now (June, 1941) considering. The methods by which the government may borrow to meet these deficits will now be examined.

COMMERCIAL BANKS

The government may sell its newly issued bonds to the commercial banks; the banks usually pay for the bonds by transferring to the government's name part of their deposits on reserve at the Federal Reserve Bank. The government then uses these deposits to pay its current expenses. In this process part of the deposits is transformed into currency, but the larger part is transferred to the commercial banks, taking the form of deposits in those banks in the name of those who have furnished the government with the materials, services, and so on. Less commonly, the commercial bank buys a bond from the government by simply writing up on its books a deposit to the account of the government. In either case, the result of the government's borrowing from the commercial banks is to increase the total volume of bank deposits compared to what they would have been if the government had raised its funds by taxation or certain other forms of borrowing. Hence this type of government borrowing increases the stock of money in the country.

Present Holdings of Government Bonds and Hypothetical Holdings.—Some quantitative relationships may now be examined. On June 29, 1940 (virtually the end of the fiscal year 1940), the commercial banks held $16.5 billion of Federal direct and guaranteed obligations.[1] The computations on page 24 above resulted in a cumulative Federal deficit for 1941–51 of $79 billion, if the tax system were not to be strengthened at all, and under the assumptions made in Table 2 with respect to expenditures. If the commercial banks were asked to buy all the $79 billion, their holdings would increase to $96 billion by 1951. These figures themselves suggest that if any such deficit were to arise, it would not be financed wholly in this manner. In any case, the illustration is useful only as a first step, since there is no chance that a deficit of that size will develop so far as the tax element is concerned; the tax system will certainly be strengthened.

Under the first set of tax changes, the cumulative deficit for 1941–51 would be about $50 billion. If this, or the corresponding $30-billion deficit for 1941–43, were covered entirely by selling bonds to commercial banks, the increase in

[1] On December 31, 1940, these holdings were $17.8 billion. These and all subsequent figures on bank assets or liabilities have been taken from the annual reports of the Comptroller of the Currency, except the December, 1940, figure, which is taken from the semiannual statement by the Comptroller of the Currency, available in a press release of the Treasury Department.

their holdings would still be far beyond what anyone is thinking of today as practicable. But it may be asked, simply to bring out the issues involved: is there any compelling reason why this could not be done?

Reserve Requirements.—There is first the question of reserves. The law requires that, for every dollar of deposits that they have outstanding (so to speak) against themselves, the banks must have a certain fraction of a dollar on deposit with the Federal Reserve Banks as "reserves." At present they have much more with the Reserve Banks than they need for the volume of deposit claims against themselves. The excess reserves, now between $5 and $6 billion, will tend to be increased as more gold flows into the country, though this flow will certainly be less than it has been in recent years. On the other hand, the banks are being called on to create money for business borrowers, and in certain other cases. Loans and investments (other than in Federal obligations) seem likely to increase by at least two billions in calendar 1941, and the next two or three years may also show substantial increases. Moreover, the excess reserves are not distributed evenly among the banks; some have a very small excess if any at all. In view of these factors, it is impossible to say by how much the banks would be able to expand the stock of money through buying Federal bonds without exhausting their excess reserves and consequently having to borrow at the Federal Reserve Banks. But it appears that less than one half of the hypothetical $50 billion in cumulative deficit (under the first set of tax changes), or not much more than two thirds of the corresponding 1941–43 deficit of $30 billion might be financed in this manner.

When the commercial banks finally came to borrow from the Federal Reserve Banks in order to buy still more government bonds, they would have to pay interest on these borrowings. The earnings of the Reserve Banks are available to meet losses, deficits, and a 6 percent cumulative dividend on the capital stock; the remainder of their earnings belong, in effect, to the Federal government, since any surplus would go to the government if the Reserve Banks were liquidated. Hence the commercial banks, at the point where their excess reserves are exhausted, can create new money only by paying what amounts in large part to a tax to the Federal government—a tax on the creation of money.

But if the government were determined to sell the entire $50 billion of bonds to the commercial banks, the reserve requirements would not stand in the way, whatever else might. The government, as represented by the Board of Governors of the Federal Reserve System, and ultimately by Congress, has the power to say how large a fraction of a dollar must be kept on reserve for each dollar of deposit. At least it can say so within limits quite wide enough for purposes of the present discussion.

Ratio of Deposits to Capital, Surplus, and Undivided Profits.—Secondly, there is the question of the ratio of deposits to capital, surplus, and undivided profits. Deposits are claims against the bank's assets; the capital, surplus, and undivided profits reflect what is left of the assets after setting off against them the deposits and any other claims against the bank; this remainder belongs to the stockholders. If the deposits got to be very large compared with the bank's capital, surplus, and undivided profits, a small percentage loss in the value of the correspondingly huge volume of assets would compel a big percentage cut in the capital, surplus, and undivided profits in order to make good on the claims represented by the deposits.

A ratio of ten dollars of deposit to one dollar of capital, surplus, and undivided profits has commonly been considered reasonable; but some banks have expanded to a much higher ratio—more than 20 to 1 in one well-known case. On June 29, 1940, the commercial banks had $34 billion of demand deposits and $16 billion of time deposits as claims against their assets (excluding deposits of one commercial bank with another commercial bank)—a total of $50 billion. By December 31, 1940, the total had risen to $55 billion. The total capital, surplus, and undivided profits of these banks on June 29, 1940, was $6.4 billion. On a strictly average, mechanical computation, using the 10-to-1 ratio, the banks would not buy more than another $10 billion or so of government bonds even if they created no new deposits for other borrowers meanwhile. To add a full $50 billion to the already existing $50 billion would result, by mid-year 1951, in deposits of $100 billion, and a deposit-to-capital ratio of 16 to 1 instead of 10 to 1. Actually, the volume of deposits would probably be even greater by that time; the banks might have been creating deposits for still other borrowers, and a continued inflow of gold might also have increased deposits correspondingly.

But the 10-to-1 ratio is, after all, only a custom; nothing mechanical, so to speak, stands in the way of letting deposits grow until the ratio rises to 15 to 1 or 20 to 1. From the banker's point of view, much depends on the proportion of his resources that are in long-term investments, hence less liquid. The problem here becomes one for the specialist in banking; would the commercial banks in fact refrain from buying government bonds because the 10-to-1 ratio—or something close to it—would have to be surpassed unless the capital account itself were increased by selling additional shares of stock in the bank? And, if so, would the capital account be thus strengthened? The present writer's impression is that the banks would not allow themselves to be stopped from creating the new deposits simply on the grounds of the ratio, if they were really eager otherwise to buy the new bonds. Moreover, new capital might be raised—from the government if not from the public—to strengthen the ratio.

Rate of Interest.—What do the considerations adduced above indicate with respect to the rate of interest at which the commercial banks would be willing to purchase new Federal bonds?

Opinions differ on this point. On the one hand, the banks undergo no great expense in creating the new money, so long as they do not have to borrow from the Federal Reserve. They undergo some expense in handling the new deposits thus created, and, more important, they must pay a fee to the Federal Deposit Insurance Corporation based on the total volume of their deposits (the banks that are uninsured account for a negligible proportion of total deposits). But to the individual bank these facts can scarcely be a deterrent. Its own increase in deposits usually comes indirectly, not as a direct result of its own purchase of the new bonds. And with respect to the cost of handling the checks drawn on the new deposits, much the same expense would be encountered if the government's policy, through taxation or other types of borrowing, resulted in turning over existing deposits more rapidly.

On the other hand, is there some premium for risk that needs to be taken into account here? Might the banks feel impelled to ask an extra percent or so as a hedge against a possibility that the government would repudiate its debt? No one can forecast just how the banks might feel about this, but in guarding against any easy assumption that such an attitude would develop, it is useful to recall that to the bank it is sufficient (generally speaking) if it gets paid off in the number of dollars that it has loaned, since the claims against the bank are likewise in dollars. And the Federal government has, in the last analysis, the power (or the power to create the power) to create dollars in unlimited amounts.

Another, more immediate, reason why the banks might soon demand higher interest rates on long-term issues is that they might anticipate the possibility that interest rates would increase somewhat in later years. Some banks may, for instance, be adopting the view that the government will at some future time be unwilling to lower the reserve requirements if that should be necessary to keep the rate down. Because of that possibility, they would be unwilling, beyond a certain point, to lock themselves into a low-rate bond for a long term. But there is evidence that some banks do not trouble to analyze the situation in these terms. Incidentally, it is now possible for depositary banks to get 2 percent for twelve years without being locked in; the new Depositary Bonds are redeemable at par and accrued interest at the option of either the government or the depositaries and financial agents.[2]

Some observers believe that a mere trend in the direction of lower excess reserves would be enough to make the banks unwilling to buy more government bonds unless they were given a somewhat higher rate of interest. It seems unlikely, however, that a reduction from, say, $6 billion to $4 billion would have much effect, in view of the absolute size of the $4 billion. Again, much would depend on what the banks thought the government would be willing to do toward decreasing the reserve requirements.

This discussion is probably too much in terms of the banks' endeavoring to make all the money they can in any way they can. Actually, it appears that many banks, perhaps most of them, regard their investment in government bonds as a temporary expedient adopted to maintain dividends at somewhat near normal levels. If loans to business

[2] These bonds "will be sold to depositary banks only in such amounts as will be required to provide an income to the banks necessary to offset the cost of the service rendered to the government." Treasury Press Release, May 27, 1941.

increased so much that the banks did not need all the income from their large holdings of government bonds in order to meet their normal dividend requirements, they might be reluctant to expand those holdings even though they could earn still more by doing so. They might even consider disposing of some of their government bonds. Commercial banks commonly regard their proper function as that of "lenders," not "investors." Therefore it is possible that, regardless of the size of their excess reserves, the banks might lose much of their present desire for government bonds.

In general, then, if the government shows no inclination to decrease the reserve requirements, it could not finance through the commercial banks more than half or even perhaps a quarter of the hypothetical eleven-year deficit of $50 billion (under the first set of tax changes) without increasing the rate of interest it would pay. And in terms of the three-year period ending June 30, 1943, not more than four fifths of the $30-billion deficit for that period (under the first set of tax changes) and perhaps indeed not more than half of it could be financed through the commercial banks without an increase in the rate of interest. But the dominant factor is the government's power to change the reserve requirements. If the government were determined to finance such deficits through the commercial banks it is at least arguable that it could do so without appreciably increasing the interest rate.

Actually, the government is showing a strong inclination to depend as little as possible on the commercial banks. It will undoubtedly sell substantial amounts to others, described below. Meanwhile, the Treasury has shown an aversion to raising the rate that it pays on that part of its debt sold to commercial banks, except to allow for the recent elimination of tax exemption.

The combination of factors involved here has led to the use of an assumption, in the present computations, that the interest rate on the bonds floated to cover the deficit will not, on the average, exceed 2.5 percent—or, in terms of the old, wholly tax-exempt bonds, about 2 percent.[8] An adjustment has been made in the computations below whenever it is assumed that the rate is placed appreciably higher than this to attract other classes of borrowers.

MUTUAL SAVINGS BANKS

The government does not wish to finance its deficit entirely through the commercial banks, if only because it prefers to obviate the creation of so much additional money. It may instead borrow from (1) mutual savings banks, (2) insurance companies, (3) other corporations, and (4) individuals (including trust funds).

Recent Experience and Possible Normal Purchases.—The mutual savings banks can be only a minor source of funds for the Federal government. On June 29, 1940, these banks had $10.6 billion in deposits. They also had $1.3 billion surplus, undivided profits, and reserves. The total amount—$12 billion, to the nearest billion—was invested almost wholly in loans on residential properties ($4.8 billion), in Federal direct and guaranteed obligations ($3.1 billion), in obligations of the states and their political subdivisions ($0.6 bil-

[8] The computed rate of interest on the total outstanding debt was 2.6 percent in December, 1940 (Treasury *Bulletin,* Jan., 1941, p. 24), but for new issues the assumption of a 2 percent rate seems not too low. An appreciable part of the banks' holdings is in short-term securities carrying low interest rates. On June 30, 1940, the insured commercial banks owned $15.9 billion of Federal direct and guaranteed securities, and, of these, $0.8 billion were in bills, $2.7 billion in notes, $0.9 billion in RFC notes, and $0.7 billion in Treasury bonds maturing within 5 years (*ibid.,* Oct., 1940, p. 22; see also *ibid.,* May, 1941, p. 1). All new obligations will be fully taxable, under the Public Debt Act of 1941, and the rate of interest may therefore be closer to 2.5 percent, but the tax estimates used here do not include the revenues that will result from this new policy; the net result may therefore still be taken, tentatively, as 2 percent—see p. 15. The spread will not, presumably, be as great as 0.5 percent, but for present purposes of rough computation it will be convenient to use 0.5 percent instead of a more refined figure.

lion), and in obligations of railroads and public utilities ($1.2 billion). One billion dollars was uninvested—held in currency or coin or deposited with other banks. Table 14 shows how some of those items have changed over the past four years. The appetite for Federal bonds grew even faster than the investable funds, from the middle of 1936 to the middle of 1938, chiefly because public utility bonds held by

TABLE 14

CHANGES IN DEPOSITS AND GOVERNMENT BOND HOLDINGS
ALL MUTUAL SAVINGS BANKS, 1936–40 [a]
(*Money Figures in Billions*)

	Number of Banks	*Direct and Guaranteed Federal Obligations*	*Obligations of States and Political Subdivisions*	*Currency and Coin and Balances with Other Banks*	*Total Deposits*	*Total Capital Accounts*
June 30, 1936	566	$2.1	[b]	$0.6	$10.1	$1.3
Dec. 31, 1936	565	2.3	[b]	0.6	10.1	1.4
June 30, 1937	564	2.4	$0.8	0.5	10.2	1.4
Dec. 31, 1937	563	2.5	0.8	0.5	10.3	1.4
June 30, 1938	562	2.7	0.7	0.6	10.2	1.3
Dec. 31, 1938	555	2.9	0.7	0.6	10.3	1.3
June 30, 1939	552	3.0	0.6	0.7	10.4	1.3
Dec. 30, 1939	551	3.1	0.6	0.8	10.5	1.3
June 29, 1940	551	3.1	0.6	1.0	10.6	1.3

[a] Comptroller of the Currency, *Annual Reports*.
[b] Not segregated.

these banks were being refunded at rates of interest so low that government bonds became increasingly attractive and because many mortgages were being repaid, with no corresponding opportunity available to invest in new mortgages. Also, the savings banks were liquidating railroad bonds that had lost their former gilt-edge character. These factors operated less strongly in the next two years, and the savings banks' holdings of Federal bonds increased as much as, but no more than, their deposits. It will be assumed here that over the next decade this one-to-one ratio will be maintained. If savers' incomes are not cut into very deeply by new taxation, the deposits might increase by $1 billion over the period 1941–51, even allowing for the sale of Savings Bonds to individuals. If, in addition, the savings banks were willing to draw somewhat on the billion dollars uninvested, they might take $1.3 billion in Federal bonds without having to sell any of their other assets in a quantity significant for the present discussion.

The rate of interest would probably not have to be higher than 2.5 percent to induce these purchases. The safety factor in Federal bonds will induce the savings banks to purchase them at an interest rate lower by about 1/4 of 1 percent than the rate on high-grade corporate bonds. The savings banks now pay from 1 percent to 2 percent on deposits. These banks are exempt from the Federal income tax, and no doubt they will tend to shift out of the old Federal bonds that are exempt from the corporation normal tax into the new taxable bonds, since the market in general sets a lower price on the latter bonds. This feature will presumably also have some influence on the total amount of Federal bonds that the savings banks will hold.

The Question of Still Heavier Purchases.—There is not much point in assuming that the savings banks will make still heavier purchases of Federal bonds by selling a substantial amount of their other assets, unless there is some reason why the government would prefer to see its bonds with the savings banks rather than with others (including the others who would use their funds in buying the assets the savings banks would have to sell).

Diversion or Withdrawal of Depositors' Funds to Purchase Government Bonds.—A substantial part of the individuals' savings that have gone into Savings Bonds in the past few years (see p. 86) would doubtless have gone into the savings banks instead. Possibly the savings banks' deposits would have increased by $200 million to $500 million more in the year ending June 30, 1940, for example, if the Savings Bonds had not been on the market. For future years this factor is taken into account, in the present computations, by assuming that the experience will parallel that of recent years. An intensified Savings Bond (now "Defense Savings Bond") campaign might make untenable the above assumption of a $1.0 billion increase in deposits in savings banks during 1941–51, but the quantity involved is probably not significant for the present analysis. In any case there is no compelling reason for the Federal government to attract this kind of money from individuals so long as the savings banks are inclined to increase their holdings of Federal bonds by at least as much as their deposits rise.

A very intense campaign to sell Defense Savings Bonds might even induce the public to withdraw a substantial portion of the $11 billion deposits now on hand. There is, however, still less reason for the government to aim at this result than there is for it to induce the banks themselves to buy bonds beyond the hypothetical $1.3 billion above. In either case the banks would have to sell assets—in the one case to let the depositor withdraw his money (transfer it to a commercial bank, in effect) to give to the government; in the other case, to get the funds itself to give to the government. It might be argued that when the public buys the bonds there is a danger that the kind of asset that the savings bank sells may be government bonds. However, the kind of asset that the savings bank sells probably does not make very much difference. In the one case the bank maintains its other types of asset, and the (old) government bond passes into the hands of the bank's vendee; in the other case the bank maintains its government bond holdings, and a part of its other assets passes into the hands of the vendee. In either case the purchaser of the savings bank's assets is correspondingly less able to buy government bonds himself; the chief difference is a shift in the distribution of those bonds. The temporary effect on the government bond market might be somewhat more unfavorable in the former case. In any event, the government would have to offer a high interest rate—possibly as high as 4 or 5 percent—to induce the public to make substantial withdrawals, as contrasted with mere diversion, of funds from the savings banks. In general, then, it seems safe to rule out this withdrawal technique as a source of funds for the government.

Effect of Tax Changes.—The savings banks would have the $1.3 billion available to invest in government bonds only if the government refrained from enacting a tax program so severe that it would seriously affect the flow of money to these banks. The first set of tax changes would probably diminish the flow somewhat; under the second set, too, the effects might be appreciable. And with all five sets in force, would there be any net flow to the savings banks at all? There seems to be no information at the moment on which to build even a rough quantitative guess, but for illustrative purposes it may be useful to assume that the savings banks would buy only $0.8 billion if the first set of tax changes were in force, $0.5 billion if the second set also were enacted, about the same if the third and fourth were also in force, and none at all if all five were operative.

INSURANCE COMPANIES

Insurance companies increased their holdings of Federal direct and guaranteed obligations from only $800 million on June 30, 1932, to $6.1 billion eight years later, according to estimates made by the Treasury Department: [4]

[4] House, Committee on Ways and Means, *Hearings, Public Debt Act of 1941*, p. 24.

June 30	*Billions of Dollars*
1932	$0.8
1933	1.0
1934	1.5
1935	2.6
1936	3.9
1937	5.0
1938	5.2
1939	5.8
1940	6.1

During the calendar year 1940, the life insurance companies purchased "about $500,000,000" of Federal securities, direct or guaranteed.[5]

The 26 largest legal reserve life insurance companies showed the following holdings of "Bonds—U. S. Govts." (this excludes states and localities) as of December 31, in billions of dollars: [6]

1929	0.3	1934	1.7
1930	0.3	1935	2.6
1931	0.3	1936	3.6
1932	0.4	1937	4.3
1933	0.8	1938	4.5

(Of the 1938 amount, the Metropolitan held $0.9 billion, the Prudential, $0.8 billion, and the New York Life, $0.6 billion.) The life insurance companies show a preference for the longer term bonds; of the $4.5 billion total (1938), $3.7 billion had a maturity of 1945 or later.[7]

These figures might suggest that in years when national income is rising rapidly, the insurance companies will add nearly a billion dollars to their Federal bond holdings, but

[5] *Federal Reserve Bulletin,* Feb., 1941, p. 92.

[6] Temporary National Economic Committee, *Hearings,* Part 10-A, pp. 98, 113.

[7] *Ibid.,* p. 140. See also Treasury *Bulletin,* May, 1941, p. 1, showing that of $5.4 billion holdings reported by 200 life insurance companies as of March 31, 1941, 69 percent were in obligations due, or first becoming callable, after 5 years.

that in depression years the increase may be little or nothing. Actually, however, this conclusion appears unjustified. In recent years the increase in holdings of Federal bonds by twenty-six life insurance companies has been much less than the increase in admitted assets. In 1936, assets increased $1.7 billion; holdings of Federal bonds, only $1.0 billion. In 1937 the respective amounts were $1.2 billion and $0.7 billion; in 1938, $1.2 billion and $0.2 billion.[8] Under their outstanding and prospective policies, the life insurance companies need to earn between 3 percent and 3.5 percent. Government bonds selling to yield 2 to 2.5 percent are therefore not attractive to the life insurance companies, even to those that pay little or no Federal income tax. There will be some shifting out of the old tax-free issues into the new taxable issues, as with the mutual savings banks, but it would be unsafe to count on further substantial increases in the insurance companies' holdings so long as the Treasury wishes to maintain a low rate of interest on its total debt outstanding. A drive to sell bonds based on a patriotic appeal might bring a substantial increase in such holdings, but it is here assumed that the Treasury will not resort to forcing bonds on anyone who does not want them. All in all, it seems best for purposes of the present computation to assume that insurance corporations absorb only $0.3 billion a year on the average over the next decade, though this figure is more likely to prove too low than too high. Yearly fluctuations above and below this amount are disregarded here.*

The government might strengthen the insurance companies as potential purchasers of its bonds by cultivating

[8] *Ibid.*, pp. 98, 113.

* As this book goes to press, it appears that this figure is much too low, owing to the growing difficulty faced by the insurance companies in getting a much higher yield from other safe sources. Perhaps $1.0 billion a year is a minimum average for the next two or three years. The amount to be absorbed by commercial banks (Table 15, l. 4) would be correspondingly less.

among the public a desire for insurance. In Canada, for instance, there has been some discussion of using the insurance companies in this manner, or at least of inducing increased withdrawal of the public's funds from spending, whether or not the insurance companies buy government bonds with the premiums.[9] It is argued that in any case the insurance companies would serve a useful purpose in draining off consumer purchasing power and to this extent preventing consumers from bidding up the price of consumers' goods.

OTHER CORPORATIONS

Other corporations held only $2.1 billion of Federal direct and guaranteed obligations on June 30, 1938; tax-exempt organizations, only $0.5 billion; and state and local government investment funds, only $0.3 billion.[10] Considering the net results of the decade 1941–51, and in view of the wide margin of error of the figures assumed for that period, it seems best to disregard those sources as potential purchasers of substantial amounts of new Federal obligations. Under a recently announced program, the Treasury is to sell Series F and Series G savings bonds to individuals, trusts, and corporations. These bonds, however, yield only 2.5 percent at the most. To the larger corporations, which pay a 24 percent normal tax (plus 6 percent surtax, under current proposals), the net yield is only 1.9 percent (or 1.75 percent)—not much more than they can get on outstanding tax-exempt Federal bonds of similar maturity. Moreover, no one purchaser may buy more than $50,000 of the F and G bonds in a year.

Priorities and other forms of control over production may induce many corporations to refrain from investing their profits in inventory expansion, plant expansion, and the like, and also to refrain somewhat from spending their deprecia-

[9] A. F. W. Plumptre, "An Approach to War Finance," *Canadian Journal of Economics and Political Science*, Feb., 1941.

[10] Temporary National Economic Committee, *Hearings*, Part 9, p. 4098.

tion funds and other moneys in keeping up their existing inventories, plant, and so on. Hence they may find themselves accumulating reserves of cash so large that they will come into the market for substantial amounts of government bonds. At the present time, however, no quantitative expression, in amounts large enough to be significant for the present rough type of analysis, can be given to this factor. Meanwhile, business corporations are to a considerable extent moving in the opposite direction by liquidating their holdings as growing inventories and the like increase their need for funds.

The states, through their unemployment trust funds, may be substantial purchasers of Federal bonds in the next few years, but they may also become substantial sellers, under the postulated depression in later years. For present purposes, with respect to the eleven-year period as a whole, the net result may be disregarded.

INDIVIDUALS

To what extent might the government expect to sell bonds to individuals—at what interest rates—without inducing them (or forcing them) to borrow the money from commercial banks to buy the bonds? If a somewhat higher interest rate than prevails on ordinary issues has to be offered to attract individual savings, how can the banks be prevented from buying them? Does the offer of such an interest rate tend to "break" the rest of the bond market?

Savings Bonds in the Past Few Years.—The experience with the Savings Bonds, first issued on March 1, 1935, is instructive on all these points. It has demonstrated the possibilities of splitting the government bond market into more or less watertight compartments, with different interest rates ruling in each. The Savings Bonds, now Defense Savings Bonds, Series E, may be purchased only by individuals (this restriction has been in force only since April 1, 1940). A single ownership of bonds issued in any one calendar year is limited to $5,000 (maturity value). These restrictions are made effective by the provision that the bonds are nontransferable. They carry no coupons, but are instead issued at a price of $75 for every $100 of maturity value, due ten years later. This is equivalent to an annual rate of interest of 2.9 percent. The holder can present his bond for redemption at an earlier date, but then gets a lower rate of return. The 2.9 percent yield is substantially higher than the market has been placing on ordinary Treasury bonds of comparable term. Thus the Treasury bonds callable June 15, 1951, were selling on April 15, 1941—approximately ten years ahead—to yield 1.8 percent.[11] There is not enough tax differential to support this difference in yield. This Treasury bond is exempt from Federal normal income tax, but the rate is only 4.4 percent on individuals. It is subject to Federal surtax except that the taxpayer is allowed an exemption from surtax with respect to the interest on a principal amount up to $5,000. The interest on the Series E Defense Savings Bonds is fully taxable. For these bonds, the "interest" is the difference between the issue price and the redemption price; and the "principal" is the issue price.[12] A taxpayer on a cash basis does not account for his interest until he redeems the bond; conceivably, this lumping up of interest into one year might throw him into a higher-rate surtax bracket and cause some slight tax disadvantage compared with the holder of the ordinary Treasury bond with coupons. And if tax rates promise to go up indefinitely, the disadvantage is accentuated. On the other hand, postponement of the tax gives the taxpayer the use of a larger earning asset meanwhile.

With one exception, each year has shown an increase in

[11] Treasury *Bulletin*, April, 1941, p. 27.

[12] *Prentice-Hall Federal Income Tax Course, 1940–1941*, pp. 202–3.

the amount of Savings Bonds sold (issue price, in millions of dollars):[13]

Fiscal Year	*Amount*
1935 (March 1 to June 30)	63
1936	264
1937	513
1938	488
1939	685
1940	1,109
TOTAL	3,120

Only $311 million (redemption value) have been presented for redemption.[14] A total of $2.9 billion were outstanding on June 30, 1940 (current redemption value).[15] Three fourths of them (on a maturity value basis) were held by individuals, 9 percent by fiduciaries, 9 percent by banks and trust companies, and 6 percent by other corporations and associations (the last three groups are no longer allowed to purchase them). Seventy percent of the Savings Bonds (on a sale price basis) were in the largest denominations—$1,000; 15 percent were $500 bonds, and 10 percent, $100 bonds.[16] And the redemptions have been consistently greater (as a proportion of the total of the denomination issued) as the bonds have been of smaller denominations. On June 30, 1940, it is estimated that there were approximately 2,000,000 owners of Savings Bonds.[17] These data suggest that the bonds have been purchased largely by members of the middle class

[13] *Report of the Secretary of the Treasury for the Fiscal Year Ended June 30, 1940*, p. 62.

[14] If the price level were allowed to get out of hand, there is the possibility—perhaps not very strong—that the government would have to meet a flood of redemptions of the Savings Bonds.

[15] This figure had risen to $3.6 billion by April 30, 1941. Treasury *Bulletin*, May, 1941, p. 16.

[16] *Report of the Secretary of the Treasury for the Fiscal Year Ended June 30, 1940*, pp. 62, 63.

[17] *Ibid.*, p. 396.

rather than the lowest income groups; perhaps virtually all of them are held by individuals with incomes large enough to make them subject to the income tax.

There is some evidence that part of the hoarded currency has been flowing into Savings Bonds. Whether this movement will continue is doubtful; no allowance is made for such a possibility here. The currency circulating outside the banks is large, but probably not large enough to permit of a flow into Savings Bonds that would materially alter the situation. Of the total $9.1 billion of paper currency and coin in circulation outside the Treasury and Federal Reserve Banks on April 30, 1941, $6.4 billion was of small denomination ($20 or less) and was perhaps not, for the most part, held as hoards.[18] Currency is being hoarded by various types of persons, it is said, including aliens who have sought to escape having their funds "frozen," individuals who are still distrustful of banks, and would-be evaders of the income tax.

Defense Savings Bonds in the Coming Decade.—With incomes rising as a result of the defense program, it appears likely that the government could continue to sell well over a billion dollars a year (issue price) of these bonds (Series E Bonds, not to be confused with the newly issued Series F and G Bonds, which, although also "Defense Bonds," are treated in a separate section below). At least, this might be so through the fiscal year 1945, if there were no drain on incomes by increases in tax rates or new taxes, and if the cost of living did not rise enough to impair seriously the margin for this type of saving; indeed, it would not be surprising if sales averaged about $2 billion. It has been pointed out in several places above that these two assumptions—no new taxes and no substantial rise in the cost of living—are presumably incompatible. Moreover, the fact is that the tax system is going to be strengthened. Still, it is useful as a first

[18] *Federal Reserve Bulletin,* June, 1941, p. 549.

step to consider what the sales of the Defense Bonds might be under those assumptions. The net sales, less redemption before maturity, might easily reach (in billions) $1, $2, $3, $2, and $1 for the fiscal years 1941–45 respectively. In May, 1941, the first month during which the Series E bonds were offered, total sales were $115 million. In June, 1941, they were $99 million.[19]

Much depends on factors whose force it is difficult to gauge at the moment. The Treasury is putting on sale Defense Savings Stamps priced at $.10, $.25, $.50, $1, and $5. They bear no interest, but can be consolidated into Defense Savings Bonds. And although the Treasury has repeatedly emphasized its determination not to promote sales under the high-pressure methods of the Liberty Loan and Victory Loan campaigns, one cannot be sure that local community sentiment will not lead to something resembling that situation. If the campaign includes the signing of pledges to purchase amounts periodically, implemented perhaps by regular deductions from payrolls (voluntarily agreed to), the sales of the Stamps and Defense Bonds could (under the assumption given) go substantially beyond the figures set down above. An increase could likewise be expected if consumer purchases were restricted by nonfiscal measures—for example, a restriction of installment financing, or price fixing coupled with widespread rationing that leaves part of one's income unspendable.

What of the sales of Series E Bonds during 1946–51? Still under the preliminary assumptions of no tax increases and no rise in the cost of living, it seems not unduly optimistic to assume that they would be sufficient to cover the maturing Savings Bonds (computed at issue value) and in addition to supply the government with, say, zero, zero, $1, $2, $2, and

[19] Treasury Press Releases, June 7, July 3, 1941. In those two months, $6 million Defense Savings Stamps were sold.

$2 billion respectively. The net effect of such sales must include a slight offset on account of the 2.9 percent rate on those bonds instead of the 2 percent that has been assumed thus far in computing the interest charge and hence the deficit. The total added interest burden for the eleven years would be less than $1 billion. For convenience in computation it may be set at $1 billion and simply offset against the $2 billion assumed for 1951 immediately above, reducing it to $1 billion. Under these assumptions, the net effect of the Series E Bonds for the period 1941–51 would be to give the government $15 billion.

To come closer to reality, it may be assumed that the first set of tax changes, or something similar, has been enacted. The increases in the surtax rates would undoubtedly curtail somewhat the purchase of Defense Bonds. Only the most general kind of guess is in order here; perhaps it might be assumed that for the entire period of eleven years the net sales (after allowing for the somewhat higher interest rate, as above), less redemptions, would cumulate to $13 billion. A further rise in surtaxes, as under the second set, might cut this to $10 billion. Use of the third and fourth sets in addition (excises and sales tax) might in each case cause a further drop of $1 billion. Use of the fifth set also (rise in payroll taxes) might have an appreciable effect, possibly allowing the government to draw a total of only $7 billion over the eleven-year period.

The unreliability of these figures needs scarcely be emphasized. Their only value is in indicating general conclusions: if no tax increases were made, the Series E Bonds, as at present issued, could not be expected to cover more than a small part of the cumulative 1941–51 deficit, even in the then unlikely event that the cost of living did not rise. If taxes were increased so greatly that the cumulative deficit for that period dropped to about $28 billion, the Series E

Bonds might not cover even one third of that deficit (which, it must be recalled, is based on estimates of expenditures that are probably not too high in the aggregate). In any case, the Defense Bonds are a factor important enough to be considered in even the roughest type of computation. And if they were sold through some forced loan program like the "deferred pay" plan discussed by Keynes,[20] these figures would have to be drastically revised.

Ordinary Treasury Obligations.—The appetite of individuals for ordinary Treasury obligations has not been keen in recent years. From June 30, 1938, to June 30, 1940, the total interest-bearing securities of the Federal government, direct and guaranteed, held outside government agencies and trust funds, rose from $36.6 billion to $40.8 billion; that is, by $4.2 billion. Meanwhile, the Federal Reserve Banks sold $0.1 billion. Thus there is $4.3 billion to be accounted for.

The Savings Bonds increased by $1.8 billion in that period.[21] The mutual savings banks increased their holdings of Treasury obligations by $0.4 billion, the commercial banks by $2.5 billion, and the insurance companies by $0.9 billion. The total of these figures is $5.6 billion. However, banks and insurance companies apparently held $0.3 billion in Savings Bonds.[22] This represents a duplication in that total, which must be lowered to $5.3 billion. Comparison of this latter figure with the $4.3-billion item shows that others—individuals, trusts, and corporations—must have decreased their holdings of ordinary Federal obligations by $1.0 billion in the two-year period. Some of this may have represented a

[20] John Maynard Keynes, *How to Pay for the War,* New York, 1940, pp. 27 ff.

[21] *Report of the Secretary of the Treasury, 1940,* p. 62.

[22] *Ibid.,* p. 95. This report shows a change in "nonmarketable" holdings of $1.5 billion instead of the $1.8 billion used above, the difference being accounted for by Savings Bonds in the hands of other investment institutions.

shift into Savings Bonds. Perhaps an allowance should be made for a further like disinvestment in the future. In the present discussion, however, it will be assumed that there will be no net investment or disinvestment in this respect. Even if some disinvestment does occur, it seems unlikely to be on a scale large enough to be significant for the present computations.

Series F and Series G Bonds.—The recently announced Series F and Series G types of Savings Bonds represent a policy between that of the 2.9 percent Savings Bonds and the ordinary Treasury bonds. Their yield to maturity is about 2½ percent, somewhat more than the Treasury bonds of like maturity (twelve years). Series F is a discount bond; Series G pays interest semiannually by check. Of importance to individuals, trusts, and corporations (commercial banks excluded), for which they are designed, is the fact that—like the Savings Bonds proper—the government stands ready to redeem them at any time at prices that guarantee against a loss of capital, no matter what happens to interest rates in general. Also, the individual investor who is emotionally conditioned against trying to pick up an ordinary Treasury bond through a brokerage house or a bank may be delighted at the chance to drop down to the post office and buy direct from the government itself.

Despite all these considerations, it seems unsafe in the present discussion to count on these new F and G bonds as a major source of funds that the government would not have obtained if they had not been issued. Corporations, as indicated above, may, in the aggregate, be out of the market for some time to come; moreover, purchases by one buyer are limited to $50,000 a year. The trust accounts are not large enough in the aggregate to affect the situation appreciably unless they resort to selling much of their present assets. The

TABLE 15

SUMMARY OF VARIOUS ASSUMPTIONS OR ILLUSTRATIONS WITH RESPECT TO BORROWING

(In Billions of Dollars)

	Present	Under First Set of Tax Changes	Under First Two Sets	Under First Three Sets	Under First Four Sets	Under All Five Sets
1. If the total increase in tax revenue, 1941–51, over what would be supplied by the tax system as it stood June 1, 1941, were	0.0	26.6	36.4	46.4	56.7	66.4
Interest saved at 2%		2.6	3.6	4.6	5.6	6.6
		29.2	40.0	51.0	62.3	73.0
2. Then the cumulative deficit, 1941–51, assuming expenditures to be about as low as seems likely, would be	79.3	50.1	39.3	28.3	17.0	6.3
3. And the loan-money available to the government, under the assumptions made in the text, would be, from these sources,						
(a) Mutual savings banks	1.3	0.8	0.5	0.5	0.5	0.0
(b) Insurance companies	3.3	3.0	2.5	2.5	2.5	2.3
(c) Other corporations; tax-exempt organizations; states and localities		(amounts are not large enough to be important for present type of computation)				
(d) Individuals: "Savings Bond" type of obligations	15.0	13.0	10.0	9.0	8.0	7.0
Total of (a) to (d)	*19.6*	*16.8*	*13.0*	*12.0*	*11.0*	*9.3*
4. Remainder—to be financed by borrowing from the commercial banks	59.7	33.3	26.3	16.3	6.0	*3.0 disinvestment*

reaction of individuals to a 2.5 percent (fully taxable) bond is at least doubtful; there is little experience yet on which to base an estimate. In May, 1941, the first month these bonds were offered, $45 million of Series F and $278 million of Series G bonds were sold.[28] In June, 1941, the respective amounts were $23 million and $147 million. Much of this, however, may represent simply a shifting of funds from ordinary Treasury obligations. For purposes of the present analysis, the Series F and G bonds will be, not ignored, but tentatively set aside as unknown factors.

SUMMARY OF ASSUMPTIONS THUS FAR WITH RESPECT TO BORROWING

Table 15 brings together the various assumptions, or illustrations of possibilities, with respect to borrowing that have been noted thus far and fills in a few gaps that were left by the discussion in the text. The figures of chief interest are probably those that show what amounts of government debt the commercial banks might be called upon to absorb over the eleven-year period. The total is $33 billion if the first set of tax changes are in force throughout the period. This is an increase of 200 percent over their present holdings. Under the first and second sets together, the increase in commercial bank holdings might be about $26 billion. With the third set of tax changes added, the amount drops to about $16 billion. And if the fourth set were added the commercial banks would increase their holdings by $6 billion. With all of the tax changes in force, a hypothetical decrease of $3 billion in commercial bank holdings of Federal bonds is obtained over the period; but it is essential to recall at once that in this last case, and probably in the one before it, the assumptions regarding national income—and hence of tax

[28] Treasury Press Releases, June 7, July 3, 1941.

revenue—would almost surely be untenable for the latter part of the decade. The same remark, with more emphasis on the first part of the decade, applies to the other extreme case, in which it is assumed that the tax system will not be strengthened at all and a figure of $60 billion added holdings is obtained. Mention of these extremes is of little use aside from indicating in a general way the quantitative aspects of certain areas bordering on the realm of reality.

Moreover, the figures of bank holdings would not in themselves be trustworthy indicators of the extent to which the stock of money would be increased or decreased, even if all the underlying assumptions were valid. Individuals, trusts, business corporations, and perhaps even savings banks and insurance companies might sell other assets in the course of absorbing the amounts of Federal bonds attributed to them in Table 15, and the commercial banks might acquire some of these assets, directly or indirectly, by an expansion of the money supply. Then, too, the commercial banks will doubtless expand that supply for some time to come by making business loans. All that the data in Table 15 can do is to sketch a tentative sort of quantitative background that may or may not prove amenable to refinement by further analysis. They serve also to point up the conclusions that (1) the amounts to be obtained in borrowing programs of the type now under consideration are dependent in part on the amount of taxation raised, but that (2) the amounts that could be raised by borrowing from others than commercial banks would not decline so fast (in absolute amount) as the tax revenue would increase under higher rates and new tax measures, although (3) the relations between this decline and this increase is an important one and needs further study, since (4) the assumptions are reasonable enough at least to indicate that the absolute amount of decline in funds available for borrowing would be far from negligible.

SALE OF BONDS TO FEDERAL RESERVE BANKS AND OTHER METHODS OF RAISING MONEY

The Federal Reserve Banks hold only $2.2 billion of Federal securities and could increase their holdings by very large amounts, either by relieving the commercial banks (or others) of some of their holdings or by buying new issues directly. Here the government possesses an instrument powerful indeed for keeping interest rates low. No quantitative data are presented on this point in these computations, however, for there are indications that the government is determined to avoid resort to the Reserve Banks. When a Federal Reserve Bank purchases a government bond, it increases not only the stock of money but also member bank reserves. Whether or not this procedure would actually lead to a greater rise in prices than would other methods of borrowing—particularly sale of new bonds direct to the commercial banks coupled with a relaxing of the reserve requirements—the fact is that such a program is commonly associated with an inflationary turn of mind. A more nearly complete study should, however, show the quantitative aspects of this possibility.

For much the same reasons, no figures will be set down in this study with respect to what might be done by issuing $3 billion of currency under the Thomas amendment, or by utilizing the gold now held in the stabilization fund, or by further devaluing the dollar. The inflationary aspects of the silver purchase plan are also excluded from the quantitative picture sketched here.

Chapter V

BORROWING AT HIGHER INTEREST LEVELS TO CHECK SPENDINGS

CREATING NEW MONEY VERSUS ACTIVATING IDLE MONEY

The kind of money that the government would get from individuals, insurance companies, and mutual savings banks under the borrowing programs considered above is very probably money that for the most part would have lain idle, or at least would have moved through the income circuit very slowly, if the government had not taken it. By far the greatest part would almost surely not have been spent in purchasing consumers' goods (food, clothing, automobiles, and so on), except possibly houses. The government would be activating idle money instead of creating and activating new money by borrowing from the commercial banks. Is there any reason to prefer one to the other? The immediate effect of the government's spending would be the same in either case, so far as the general level of prices is concerned. Indeed, the government may find itself unable to make an effective choice between the creation of new money and the activating of old. In trying to do the one, it may do the other. In borrowing from an individual, it may be leading him to sell some stocks or bonds that are then picked up, at once or later, by a bank, which expands its credit for that purpose. The converse is much less probable: if the government intended to sell its bonds to commercial banks and hence increase the stock of money, the savings banks and insurance companies, with no other outlet for their funds, might conceivably bid the new government bonds away from the commercial banks, either directly or after the banks had purchased them. In any case, the government will make a conscious choice between creating new money and speeding up the circulation of old, even though it lacks the power fully to enforce its wishes.

Indirectly, there may be somewhat more danger of a disruptive rise in the price level if the new money policy is followed than if an attempt is made to increase the velocity of circulation of the existing money. On the grounds that nothing important is to be lost by avoiding the creation of new money, and something may be gained, there is an understandable tendency to favor the activating of idle money.

DRAWING MONEY AWAY FROM THE SPENDING STREAM

But the more important issue, for the next few years, is whether the government shall activate idle money (or create new money) or instead draw in money that would otherwise have been spent—spent either in buying consumers' goods or producers' goods (for example, machines, factories, raw materials). Only by drawing in money that would otherwise have been spent can the government check whatever tendency to a price rise it may be producing by its own spending program.

1. *By Taxation.*—How can the government draw in such money? Taxation is the traditional instrument, but it is by no means a certain one. At least some of the increased tax will be paid out of money that would otherwise have lain idle or would have moved very slowly through the income circuit. Virtually no information exists on the extent to

which that may be so. About the only information bearing on the point is of a negative sort—it seems evident that families with a yearly income of less than about $1,500 will not pay much tax out of money that would otherwise have remained idle, for they have virtually none of that kind of money; at least, as a group they have none. With respect to incomes above, say, $10,000, it may appear obvious that increased taxes will come largely out of idle or slow-moving money, but there are some signs to the contrary. The mere threat of higher taxes to come may cause some of the well-to-do taxpayers to cut their standard of living somewhat, chiefly by discharging servants, closing country houses, cutting down on hospitality, resigning from clubs, and traveling less.[1] They may also forego investments (other than government bonds) that would have resulted in expenditures for producers' goods. Moreover, a net income of $10,000 is an income of only about $9,000 after deducting present Federal and state income taxes, and the possibility of meeting still further tax increases out of idle money is correspondingly reduced. This point is especially important in considering how those at much higher income levels would react to an increase in tax. A net income of $100,000 is, to a married couple with no dependents, a "disposable income"—income less present Federal income tax—of about $57,000, and still less after a state income tax.

By Borrowing.—As with taxation, a borrowing program may or may not draw to the government some money that would otherwise have been spent in the time period in question. Whether it does so or not depends chiefly on two things: (1) the rate of interest offered and (2) the degree of persuasion (or coercion) used.

[1] For an illuminating, though fragmentary, picture of the consumption habits of the wealthy, see the 100 replies received from 2,000 questionnaires sent to butlers by the Butlers Club, Inc., in 1938 (available from the magazine *Town and County*).

What are the quantitative aspects of an attempt to borrow money that would otherwise have been spent? Until a fairly detailed survey has been made, no reliable answer is possible. But the chances seem strong that little of this kind of money will be reached by offering only 3 percent, without "drives" or coercion or active assistance from labor unions and employers, including agreements by wage earners to purchase bonds periodically through payroll deductions. General observation suggests that the money the government will get at 3 percent or less is money that would otherwise have lain idle in commercial banks (either as demand or time deposits), or would have been deposited in or left in mutual savings banks, or perhaps would have been hoarded in the form of currency. Consequently, it will be useful to explore some of the quantitative results of a higher rate of interest. What, for instance, would be the effect on the annual interest charge, and hence on the deficit itself, if a 5 percent rate, tax-free basis, were offered to individuals?

In part, this discussion is concerned with possibilities rather than near-future probabilities. The government at present shows no disposition to bid above 3 percent for money, idle or active; Congress has limited the Treasury to a maximum of 3 percent on the new savings certificates authorized in the Public Debt Act of 1941 and on the Defense Savings Bonds. Among obvious reasons for this attitude is perhaps a fear that a higher rate of interest on new bonds would cause the prices of outstanding Treasury bonds —and perhaps Treasury notes—to fall, since the holders of these low-interest obligations would be inclined to sell them, even at a loss, in order to get money with which to buy the new high-interest obligations. This tendency could be greatly lessened if the new high-rate bonds were made salable only to individuals, since individuals hold a minor, though by no means negligible, proportion of the total Treasury bonds and notes outstanding.[2] The amount of these bonds and notes that would be thrown on the market by individuals might be readily absorbed by the commercial banks, especially since the latter would have been correspondingly cut off from direct purchase of bonds from the government. And since the larger part of these low-interest bonds and notes held by individuals is presumably in the hands of the well-to-do, the tendency to switch would be further repressed by setting a limit on the amount of high-interest Savings Bonds that one individual could obtain each year. The high-rate bonds would, of course, have to be made nontransferable and unavailable as collateral for bank loans.

More serious might be the switching by those who had already bought Savings Bonds at the 2.9 percent yield and the Series F and Series G Bonds at 2.5 percent. They would consider presenting the old Savings Bonds for redemption, to put the proceeds in the new high-rate bonds. A device that greatly lessens the desire to switch has, however, been incorporated in all these Savings Bonds. The effective rate of interest is made very low if the bonds are presented for redemption much before maturity. The converse of this is that, once an investor has held his Savings Bond for several years, the effective yield from that point of time to the maturity date is very high, which of course discourages switching to a new investment. For example: if a purchaser of a Defense Savings Bond holds it for six and a half years, he then finds that the yield to maturity, based on the amount of money he could get at that time if he presented it for

[2] Individuals, trusts and corporations (other than banks) apparently account for virtually all of the "other holders" who were reported to hold $9.7 billion of marketable Federal issues on June 30, 1940. No figures are available on trust holdings. For corporations, see p. 83. *Report of the Secretary of the Treasury, 1940*, p. 95.

TABLE 16

CHANGES IN DEFICIT, UNDER ASSUMPTION OF FIRST TWO SETS OF TAX CHANGES, THROUGH USE OF 5 PERCENT INTEREST RATE INSTEAD OF 2 PERCENT

	Interest at 2%	*Interest at 5%*	*Increase in Interest* [a]	*Deficit Computed at 2%*	*Deficit Computed at 5%*
1941	$1.0	$1.0	$0.0	$ 4.3	$ 4.3
1942	1.2	1.4	0.2	11.0	11.2
1943	1.4	2.0	0.6	12.9	13.5
1944	1.5	2.4	0.9	1.3	2.2
1945	1.5	2.4	0.9	−0.8	0.1
1946	1.6	2.5	0.9	1.9	2.8
1947	1.6	2.7	1.1	4.7	5.8
1948	1.7	3.0	1.3	4.8	6.1
1949	1.8	3.2	1.4	0.9	2.3
1950	1.8	3.3	1.5	0.3	1.8
1951	1.8	3.3	1.5	−1.5	0.0
TOTAL	$16.9	$27.2	$10.3	$39.8 [b]	$50.1

[a] Computations were made after deducting, from the deficit, interest previously computed at 2 percent. To the interest on the previously outstanding debt was then added for each fiscal year the interest at 5 percent on the increase in the deficit for the *previous* fiscal year plus one half of the interest at 5 percent on the increased deficit for the current fiscal year, on the assumption of a steady rise in the deficit over the fiscal period.

[b] The slight difference between this and the total of $39.4 billion in Table 13 represents a refinement in handling the 1942 interest charge, not important enough to justify revising all the interest and deficit data presented in Table 13 and elsewhere.

redemption, is 4.36 percent. The corresponding figure for a Series F Bond is 3.30 percent; for a Series G Bond, 3.26 percent.[3]

To avoid any possibility of overstating the added interest burden that would result from a change to a high-interest policy, it will be assumed in the following computations that the new interest rate applies only to Defense Savings Bonds

[3] For a complete table of similar figures, see Lucile Tomlinson, "Defense Bonds as Investments," *Barron's*, March 31, 1941, p. 18.

issued after June 30, 1941. The 1941 deficit will be omitted from consideration here, as the financing for that year has already been carried through.

Assuming an Interest Rate of 5 Percent on New Bonds Sold to Individuals.—The computations under an assumption of 5 percent[4] on new debt will be limited here to one case: where the first two sets of tax changes—or something approximating them—are in force. This case is selected because the current tax proposals now before Congress are fairly close to it, with respect to total amount of added tax revenue to be raised. Over the three-year period 1942–44, under the assumptions used in the present study, the cumulated interest charge for that period becomes $5.8 billion instead of $4.1 billion under a 2 percent rate—an increase of $1.7 billion. For the eleven-year period as a whole, the increase in the cumulated interest charge is $10.3 billion. The annual interest charge in 1951 would be $3.3 billion—almost twice the $1.8 billion computed under the assumption of a 2 percent rate. These figures, it will be recalled, assume that the 5 percent rate affects only that part of the debt (not including refundings) issued after June 30, 1942. The amounts involved are large enough to make it clear that, once the view is lengthened beyond the next two or three years, the size of the interest rate can readily be a matter of considerable concern.

The desirability of incurring this extra expense would depend largely on the extent to which the higher interest rate could draw in money that would otherwise have been spent and thus how much it could obviate the alternatives, which are (1) the creation of new money (borrowing from com-

[4] Actually, perhaps closer to 6 percent, assuming the bonds to be fully taxable. The reason for carrying through the present computations on an equivalent tax-free basis are given in footnote 4 in Chapter I.

mercial banks) and (2) the speeding up of the circulation of existing money. Conceivably, the use of a 5 percent rate might actually increase the use of these alternatives: it might draw in somewhat less than $10 billion in money that would otherwise have been spent, while itself creating the necessity for finding an additional $10 billion to cover the added interest charge. But this seems unlikely. And the problem raised by the $10 billion of added interest might be postponed by issuing all of the 5 percent bonds just as Savings Bonds are issued, that is, without coupons; all the interest is paid in a lump sum when the bonds mature. Then nothing would have to be paid out for interest on the debt issued to cover the 1942–51 deficit until, say, 1952, if the bonds were for ten years. This convenient way of dismissing the problem in an analysis that limits itself to 1951 is significant only for one point: the discount bond does tend to prevent the interest from being added to all the other income available for spending (and hence available for bidding prices up) during the critical period through 1945 when productive facilities, under the assumptions used here, are being strained anyway. And it may be that even over the long run of several decades the discount bond, as compared with the income bond, results in less spending, of the interest, on consumers' goods. The bondholder who might not hesitate to spend on current consumption the interest he receives by clipping a bond coupon every six months or year may easily decide to save at least part of the interest element in the lump sum of principal-repayment plus accumulated interest for ten years that he gets on the maturity of the discount bond. For every $100 that he has put in, the investor would receive $163 ten years later (5 percent compounded semiannually). Is it not unlikely that he would at once spend $63 of the $163, unless he were planning to spend all of it (as on the maturing of an education fund) or unless he had purchased small amounts so regularly that their redemption gave the appearance of a steady income stream?

The computations that have been made under the 5 percent rate rest on the assumption that at 5 percent the Treasury could get the entire $50 billion over the eleven years (excepting fiscal 1941) from individuals, and from anyone else that it might be willing to borrow from on that basis, without turning at all to the commercial banks. This assumption, though almost surely invalid, is again useful as a first step in computation; the $10 billion extra deficit resulting from the use of 5 percent is thus seen to be an outside figure, given the basic tax and expenditure assumptions. To the extent that the government failed to get its money through the 5 percents, it could turn to the commercial banks and (within the limitations noted in Chapter IV) get the remainder at 2 percent. The failure to draw so much money out of the spending stream would be partly offset by the low interest charges and a consequently smaller deficit.

Moreover, the computations of the 5 percents have omitted another vital step: an estimate that would show how much of the borrowing at 5 percent represented a real check in spending by the public, and how much of it was on the other hand reflected simply in a faster turnover of money, with little or no check to spending. Suppose that the full $50 billion was obtained from individuals by the 5 percents; we know—or rather have assumed—that $10 billion would have come anyway at 3 percent, chiefly as money that would otherwise have lain idle. And no doubt some of the remaining $40 billion would be the same kind of money—money too strongly attached to idleness to be budged at 3 percent, but detachable at various levels between 3 percent and 5 percent.[5]

The present study cannot make even the roughest estimates on the points raised in the two preceding paragraphs; the analysis must, indeed, for the present be left hanging in mid-air. The immediate purpose is served if a few of the quantitative relationships that must be studied are called to mind. These are typical of the relationships that must be blocked out, and filled in somehow or other by estimates or guesses, if a logical, internally consistent fiscal policy is to be developed.

[5] For convenience in exposition, the term "idle money" is used frequently; it is intended to include also money that is moving through the income circuit slowly. The whole concept is one of degree, and it embraces the speed of circulation of the entire money stock, including that in the hands of the government.

Appendix I

HIGHER EXPENDITURE LEVELS

IF THE ASSUMPTIONS made on page 13 concerning the outcome of the war prove too optimistic, Federal expenditures will reach levels higher than those used in the present analysis, even if the price indices do not rise appreciably above the levels assumed in Table 3. A statement of hypothetical tax revenues and deficits was drawn up, under these less optimistic assumptions, in the early stages of this study, but it appeared impracticable to shape them up for publication at this time. Some indication of the kind of results that might be obtained (on paper) is given by the basic assumptions on Federal expenditures under this more pessimistic approach: national defense rising to a peak of $15 billion for 1943–46 inclusive, aid to Britain and others rising to a $12-billion peak in 1945 and 1946, work relief and public works reaching $7 billion in 1949, and all other expenditures climbing steadily to nearly $8 billion in 1951. Total Federal expenditures exclusive of interest would reach a hypothetical maximum of $34 billion in 1946, never dropping below $20 billion a year after 1941. Tax revenues would be higher than under the other basic assumptions, since maximum business activity would be prolonged into 1946. Annual revenues under the present (June, 1941) system would be almost $15 billion in 1945–47 inclusive. Annual deficits, under these assumptions, would fluctuate between $14 billion and $22 billion, totaling $185 billion for the eleven years. These figures are obviously unreal. Long before that cumulative deficit reached its peak it would have smashed the assumptions on which it was based.

Appendix 2

COMPUTING THE FEDERAL DEBT AS OF JUNE 30, 1940, AND THE ANNUAL INTEREST CHARGES, 1941–51

THE OUTSTANDING direct Federal debt consists of the interest-bearing debt, the matured debt on which interest has ceased, and debt bearing no interest. The latter two items are small: they were $205 million and $386 million, respectively, on June 30, 1940.[1]

The interest-bearing debt ($42.4 billion on June 30, 1940)[2] is divided into public issues and special issues. The special issues totaled $4,775,000,000 on June 30, 1940, and were held chiefly by the Federal Old-Age and Survivors Insurance Trust Fund ($1.7 billion), the Unemployment Trust Fund for the states ($1.7 billion), the Government Life Insurance Fund ($0.5 billion) and the Government Retirement Funds ($0.6 billion). The Postal Savings System, the Railroad Retirement Account, and the Federal Deposit Insurance Corporation each held less than $100 million but more than $50 million of these special issues. The Adjusted Service Certificate Fund held $11 million. For present purposes, it is not desirable to include in the public debt total that amount of Federal bonds held by the Federal government itself (or its wholly owned agencies), which, when liquidated to meet out-payments to the public in later years, will be reflected as an expense item in Table 2 above. Consequently the holdings of the Old-Age Fund ($1,738,000,000) may be subtracted, leaving $3.0 billion to be counted.

[1] Treasury *Bulletin,* January, 1941, p. 16.
[2] *Idem.*

Some of the public issues are held by government-owned or government-controlled corporations, but no subtraction need be made for present purposes, since all of these appear to be extra-budgetary holdings; that is, outpayments to the public represented by liquidation would not be reflected as expenses in Table 2 above. The total amount of public issues outstanding on June 30, 1940, was $37.6 billion. If to this are added the $3.0 billion of special issues and the $0.6 billion of non-interest-bearing debt, a direct debt total, for present purposes, of $41.2 billion is obtained.

The securities guaranteed by the Federal government totaled $5.5 billion as of June 30, 1940. Here, too, government agencies and trust funds held a portion—$0.3 billion—but most of these government holdings were in the hands of the Postal Savings System and the Federal Savings and Loan Insurance Corporation,[3] and should not be excluded for present purposes.

Added to the direct-debt figure of $41.2 billion above, this gives a total Federal debt of $46.7 billion as of June 30, 1940.

The interest item in the Federal Budget may be adjusted for present purposes by subtracting the interest on the special issues held by the Old-Age Fund. Since some of these issues pay 2½ percent but most 3 percent, and since they average about $2 billion for fiscal 1941,[4] a subtraction of slightly more than $50 million is justified. Since all figures are rounded off to the nearest tenth of a billion dollars in the present computations, in Table 2 the Budget estimates for interest are reduced by a tenth of a billion dollars for fiscal 1941 and again for fiscal 1942.

The annual interest charge on the guaranteed debt is evidently little if at all above $100 million, judging from the rates of interest on the various portions of that debt.[5] Since this is covered by receipts of the issuers of this debt,[6] it is not included in the totals in Table 2, which are used primarily to ascertain the size of deficits that must be met by added taxation or borrowing.

[3] Treasury *Bulletin*, October, 1940, p. 24.

[4] Thus on January 31, 1941, there were $1.4 billion of 3 percents and $0.6 billion of 2½ percents in the Old-Age Fund (Treasury Department, *Statement of the Public Debt of the United States, January 31, 1941*).

[5] *Ibid.*

[6] About half of the $100 million is accounted for by the HOLC issues, and this was more than covered by interest receipts in fiscal 1940. See *Eighth Annual Report, Federal Home Loan Bank Board*, p. 151.

BIBLIOGRAPHY

THE FOLLOWING selected bibliography of recent writings on defense financing or war financing is designed to assist the reader who may wish to supplement the quantitative discussion of the present volume with analyses of the qualitative aspects of various policies.

Angell, James W., J. K. Galbraith, Albert Gailord Hart, Carl Shoup, and Alvin H. Hansen. "Defense Financing and Inflation: Some Comments on Professor Hansen's Article," *The Review of Economic Statistics,* May, 1941.

"Billions for Defense," *Annals of the American Academy of Political and Social Science,* March, 1941.

Bloch, Henry Simon. "Borrowing for National Defense," *Tax Magazine,* May, 1941.

Brown, F. A., J. D. Gibson, and A. F. W. Plumptre. War Finance in Canada. Toronto, Ryerson, 1940. 109 pp.

Cassel, G. "The Significance of State Borrowing in Wartime," *Quarterly Review,* Skandinaviska Banken, July, 1940.

Council for Democracy. Financing Defense. New York, 1941. 41 pp.

Crowther, Geoffrey. Ways and Means of War. Oxford, 1940. 184 pp.

Durbin, E. F. M. How to Pay for the War. London, Routledge, 1939. 119 pp.

Eccles, Marriner S. "Economic Preparedness for Defense and Post Defense Problems," *Federal Reserve Bulletin,* January, 1941.

———"Price Fixing Is Not Enough," *Fortune,* August, 1941.

"Exploring the Factors Involved in Reëmployment of Labor and Capital," *Savings Bank Journal,* December, 1940.

Fairchild, Fred Rogers, "How Can We Best Pay for Defense?" *Bulletin of the National Tax Association,* March, 1941.

———Gerhard Colm, and Discussants. "Financial Policy and the Sinews of War" and "Fiscal Policy and Recovery," *Proceedings*, National Tax Association, 1940.

Ford, Robert S. Financing National Defense. Ann Arbor, University of Michigan, 1941. 28 pp.

Gainsbrugh, Martin R., and Harlow D. Osborne. Consumption, Savings and Defense Financing. New York, National Industrial Conference Board, September 5, 1940. 8 pp.

Gilbert, Donald W. "A Tool for War-Boom Control," *Tax Magazine*, May, 1941.

Greer, Guy. "Arming and Paying for It," *Harper's Magazine*, November, 1940.

Groves, Harold M., and Others. "How to Pay for Defense," *New Republic*, Special Section, July 29, 1940.

Haensel, Paul. "War Taxation," *Taxes*, February, 1941.

Hansen, Alvin H. "Defense Financing and Inflation Potentialities," *The Review of Economic Statistics*, February, 1941.

——— "Monetary and Fiscal Controls in War Time," *Yale Review*, December, 1939.

Hardy, C. O. Wartime Control of Prices. Washington, Brookings, 1940. 216 pp.

Hart, A. G. Economic Policy for Rearmament. University of Chicago, 1940. 36 pp.

Kähler, Alfred. "The Prospects of Inflation," *Social Research*, May, 1941.

Keynes, John Maynard. *How to Pay for the War*. New York, 1940. 88 pp.

Kimmel, Lewis H., and Discussants. "The Effects of War-Time Control on Taxable Capacity," *Proceedings*, National Tax Association, 1940.

Lutz, Harley L. Financing the Defense Program. National Economy League, 1941. 22 pp.

Moulton, Harold G. Fundamental Issues in National Defense. Washington, Brookings, January, 1941. 32 pp.

Musgrave, Richard A. "Inflationary Dangers of the Public Debt and the Tax System," *Taxes*, February, 1941.

Nugent, Rolf. Guns, Planes, and Your Pocketbook. New York, Public Affairs Committee, 1941. 31 pp.

Office for Emergency Management. Defense: One Year. Washington, 1941. 30 pp.

Pigou, A. C. "War Finance and Inflation," *Economic Journal,* December, 1940.

—— The Political Economy of War. New York, 1941. 169 pp.

Plumptre, A. F. W. "An Approach to War Finance," *Canadian Journal of Economics and Political Science,* February, 1941.

Shultz, W. J. Fiscal Possibilities for National Defense. New York, National Industrial Conference Board, September 21, 1940. 8 pp.

Staudinger, Hans, and Fritz Lehmann. Germany's Economic Mobilization for War. New York, National Industrial Conference Board, July 24, 1940.

Steiner, George A. "Federal Fiscal Policy in National Defense," *Tax Magazine,* June, 1941.

Stewart, Maxwell. How Shall We Pay for Defense? New York, Public Affairs Committee, 1941.

Tax Foundation. "Objectives in Defense Financing," *Tax Review,* May, 1941.

Walker, E. Ronald. War-time Economics, with Special Reference to Australia. Melbourne University Press, 1939. 171 pp.

Williams, John H. "Economic and Monetary Aspects of the Defense Program," *Federal Reserve Bulletin,* February, 1941.

INDEX

Bei Fragen zur Produktsicherheit wenden Sie sich bitte an:
If you have any questions regarding product safety,
please contact:

Walter de Gruyter GmbH
Genthiner Straße 13
10785 Berlin
productsafety@degruyterbrill.com